W. H. DAVIES
SELECTED POEMS

JONATHAN BARKER was born in Cheltenham, Gloucester-shire, in 1949 and grew up in Bushey, Hertfordshire. Since 1973 he has been Librarian of the Arts Council Poetry Library in London. He has published critical articles and reviews in *Agenda, P. N. Review, Poetry Wales,* and the *Times Literary Supplement.* He is married and lives in London.

W. H. DAVIES

SELECTED POEMS

Chosen with an Introduction by
Jonathan Barker

William H. Davies.

OXFORD UNIVERSITY PRESS
1985

Oxford University Press, Walton Street, Oxford OX2 6DP

London Glasgow New York Toronto
Delhi Bombay Calcutta Madras Karachi
Kuala Lumpur Singapore Hong Kong Tokyo
Nairobi Dar es Salaam Cape Town
Melbourne Auckland

and associated companies in
Beirut Berlin Ibadan Mexico City Nicosia

Oxford is a trade mark of Oxford University Press

Introduction, chronology, and selection © Jonathan Barker 1985

This selection first published 1985 by Oxford University Press

British Library Cataloguing in Publication Data
Davies, W. H. (William Henry), 1871–1940
Selected poems.——(Oxford paperbacks)
I. Title   II. Barker, Jonathan, 1949–
821'.912   PR6007.A8
ISBN 0–19–281432–X

Set by Wyvern Typesetting Ltd.
Printed in Great Britain by
The Guernsey Press Co. Ltd.
Guernsey, Channel Islands

CONTENTS

from *Songs of Joy and Others* (Fifield, 1911)

from *Foliage: Various Poems* (Elkin Mathews, 1913)

* also included in *Raptures* (Beaumont Press, 1918)

xi

* also included in *The Lovers' Song-Book* (Gregynog Press, 1933)

* also included in *The Lovers' Song-Book* (Gregynog Press, 1933)

ACKNOWLEDGEMENTS

I WOULD like to thank Sandra Anstey, Cary Archard, Peter Khoroche, Martin Seymour-Smith, Jacky Simms, Will Sulkin, and David Wright for their encouragement and interest while I was preparing this selection of the poems of W. H. Davies; also Geoffrey Soar of the Little Magazines Collection, University College London, and Deborah Singmaster for her assistance in the preparation of the typescript. I am grateful to the following libraries for providing texts of the poems: the Arts Council Poetry Library, the British Library, Reference Division, and the University of London Library, Senate House. Most of all, of course, thanks to my wife Deirdre for her help and patient attention throughout.

INTRODUCTION

The Autobiography of a Super-Tramp must be one of the best, and best known, autobiographies to have been written in modern times. Like all classics it speaks as clearly to readers today as it did when first published, and the title, as with Robert Graves's *Goodbye to All That*, is known to many who have never read the book. Similarly, when we turn to W. H. Davies's poems, we find that most poetry readers will know at least one or two of them—'The Kingfisher' perhaps, or 'Leisure' with its celebrated opening lines: 'What is this life if, full of care,/We have no time to stand and stare.' But how many know that, apart from these lyrical meditations on the loveliness of the natural world, Davies wrote well over 700 poems published in 20 individual books? Good as they are, Davies's regularly anthologized poems represent only one aspect of a large body of work which displays a notable range in both subject matter and formal artistic skill.

In his lifetime Davies was a truly popular poet. His books sold well and were reprinted. He appealed to that elusive person, the common reader, who has since deserted poetry for prose and been replaced, to some extent, by the dedicated student of literature—a type of reader who tends to shun the 'popular'. So, ironically, it may be that Davies's very ability to communicate with a wide audience has contributed to his poetry falling from view. Nor, of course, given this ease of communication, do the poems require extensive critical exegesis, and it is only recently that we have woken up to the fact that some of the finest poets of this century—A. E. Housman, Edward Thomas, Thomas Hardy, Rudyard Kipling, Patrick Kavanagh, and Philip Larkin among them—while rewarding critical attention, can communicate successfully on most levels without it.

Davies has given us sufficient information in his autobiographical trilogy to satisfy even the intense contemporary interest in writers' lives. *The Autobiography of a Super-Tramp* tells of his early life in Newport and of his wanderings in America and Britain as a young man. *Later Days*, the sequel, which tells of his life in London as an author and of the writers and painters he knew, ends when he meets his future wife. *Young Emma*, written in 1924 for anonymous publication, gives us a more accurate account of his 1922 illness than the version at the end of *Later Days*, and describes how he met his wife, and their first married days together.

William Henry Davies was born in Newport, Monmouthshire, Wales, in 1871. His father died when William was three years old and the three young Davies children were brought up by their grandparents who, for a period, ran the Church House Inn. Davies left school at 14 and about a year later became apprenticed to a picture-framer and gilder. By the age of 20 he had completed his apprenticeship, lived rough in London, worked in Bristol, and had begun to take himself seriously as a poet. After the death of his grandparents he sailed for America where he travelled the country, alternately working and tramping. He made several subsequent trips across the Atlantic by cattle-ship. In 1899 he lost his right foot jumping a train in Canada and had to have the leg amputated above the knee. He returned to Newport and then moved to London, determined to continue his self-education and concentrate on writing poetry, while living cheaply in lodging houses on a small income from his grandmother's estate. In spite of his wooden leg, he still managed occasional tramps around the country.

By 1905 Davies had scraped together enough money to pay for the printing of his first book, *The Soul's Destroyer and Other Poems*. It appeared under the imprint 'Of the Author, Farmhouse, Marshalsea Road, S.E.', and was sent to reviewers and potential purchasers. The book was reviewed by Edward Thomas, among others, and soon acquired a reputation. It was Thomas who encouraged Davies to write *The Autobiography of a Super-Tramp*, published in 1908 with a preface by George Bernard Shaw. In 1911 Davies was granted a small Civil List pension and sometime around 1914 he moved to London. True to his wandering nature, even in London Davies moved from one lodgings to another, his longest stay at any one place being the six years he stayed at 14 Great Russell Street. By 1922 he had met Helen Matilda Payne. They were married in 1923 and went to live in East Grinstead. For the rest of his life Davies was content to live away from London, observing the 'green world' of his own back garden, or strolling in the nearby countryside. By the beginning of the 1930s, he and his wife had moved to Nailsworth in the Cotswolds, where they lived until Davies's death in 1940.*

In *Later Days* Davies wrote, 'I seldom stay more than five years in one place, and sometimes much less, after which I like a change of people and scenery.' This restlessness never left him, even in Nailsworth he moved house four times. When confronted with the chronology of his peripatetic life, it is all too easy to forget that Davies was a man with a handicap whose physical courage and energy were matched only by his commitment to literature, and his intellectual and creative industry.

The personality of W. H. Davies comes across most vividly in his autobiographical writings which express his thoughts, motives, and feelings with compelling honesty and directness. They show no evidence of outside influences and exhibit something of the quality described by Keats as 'negative capability' which in Davies's case takes the form of an objectivity so deeply entrenched that some readers may at times find it disturbing—as when he reports on a lynching he has witnessed, or comments on the loss of his foot:

Even then I did not know what had happened, for I attempted to stand, but found that something had happened to prevent me from doing this. Sitting down in an upright position, I then began to examine myself, and now found that the right foot was severed from the ankle. This discovery did not shock me as much as the thoughts which quickly followed. For, as I could feel no pain, I did not know but what my body was in several parts, and I was not satisfied until I had examined every portion of it.

George Bernard Shaw expresses the reaction of many readers when he remarks, 'Even as it is, I ask myself with some indignation whether a man should lose a limb with no more to-do than a

* For more detailed information on Davies's life, see the Chronology, pp. xxxiii–xlvi.

lobster loses a claw or a lizard his tail, as if he could grow a new one at his next halting place!' Davies's objectivity arose from his acceptance of life and events, whatever their impact on him.

The years Davies spent as a young man in cheap lodgings and doss-houses had made him familiar with urban squalor and scenes such as the one he describes in 'Saturday Night in the Slums': 'here was hell last night to play,/The scream of children, murder cries.' It was these experiences that made him value so highly the simple pleasures of rural life and delight in the innocence of children; 'In the Country' begins: 'This life is sweetest; in this wood/I hear no children cry for food.' To Davies's early tramping days must also be attributed the Orwell-like reportage of 'The Heap of Rags' and 'The Sleepers', as must his profound, if at times chilly, humanity.

In addition to his autobiographical trilogy, Davies wrote a number of prose books and a few other short prose pieces. His introduction to an edition of Daniel Defoe's *Moll Flanders* (Simpkin, Marshall, Hamilton, Kent & Co., 1924) contains a passage on Defoe's prose style which could equally well be applied to his own:

It is one steady march of monosyllables, without a cry of surprise or the least attempt to become eloquent. But what strength there is in these little words of his, and how they reach the heart time after time; whether he describes how the people, in the Plague of London, sat on their doorsteps and died, or relates this strange and human life of Moll Flanders. Surely it is impossible to believe that Defoe's bare and quiet style is due to a lack of strong feeling—we would rather think it due to an intensity of feeling.

Similarly, Davies's introduction to the poems of his early favourite, Robert Burns (Collins' Clear-Type Press, 1925), affords insights into his own attitude to poetry:

In reading modern poets, we are often confounded as to what kind of men they are. There is no personality in their work, and no personal confession; and though they live in London, they prefer to mention Babylon. Thinking certain subjects are hackneyed, such as love and the moon, they write obscurely on other things, forgetting that every poet who is really great makes his own moon, and gives it an entirely new beauty. They are only English in language—God only knows what nationality they are in their vision! But no man needs to be told that Burns was a Scotchman; and there is many a thought such as 'Man was made to mourn,' and 'A man's a man for a' that'—to prove that he belonged to the common people.

Finally, in the introduction to his wide-ranging anthology, *Shorter Lyrics of the Twentieth Century: 1900–1922* (Poetry Bookshop, 1922), Davies states his belief in the inescapable connection between a poet's life and his writing, echoing Ben Jonson's moral conviction expressed in the Epistle to *Volpone*, of 'the impossibility of any man's being the good poet without first being a good man', but taking the sentiment to a humorous conclusion of which Jonson would probably have approved:

There are quite a number of poets at the present time who are writing descriptive verse of a high order, which is to be seen in most of our anthologies. But their work begins and ends in description, and neither casts any light on their own minds nor on humanity in general. These poets seem to lead easy and placid lives, without having any burning sympathies to make themselves great as men. A man can be a great man without being a great poet, but I doubt whether there was ever a great poet who was not a great man. Most of these men are teetotallers, I believe, and lack the sympathy and generosity of men that drink.

Apart from Davies's well-known dictum that everyone should find time to 'stand and stare', he had little use for theorizing on poets or the writing of poetry, and this is what makes these rare asides particularly illuminating in the context of his own work.

When Davies was writing his first poems both Tennyson and Browning were still alive; Ernest Dowson, Lionel Johnson, and Arthur Symons, the poets of the nineties, were as yet unknown. By 1905, when his first book was published, A. E. Housman, W. B. Yeats, Robert Bridges, Rudyard Kipling, William Watson, and Thomas Hardy were the poets of the day. Although some of Davies's realistic poems recall John Davidson's 'Thirty Bob a Week', and others Kipling's bold directness of address, he does not seem to have been influenced by any of his contemporaries. Nor are these early poems indebted to any of the great Victorian poets; the only unmistakable echo is of Wordsworth—in 'The

Rill' and 'The Soul's Destroyer', a long poem in blank verse on the subject of drink which shares its setting with Book 7 of *The Prelude*.

> One morning I awoke with lips gone dry,
> The tongue an obstacle to choke the throat . . .
> With limbs all sore through falling here and there
> To drink the various ales the Borough kept
> From London Bridge to Newington . . .

Language which is plain, direct, and clumsily effective. Again in 'The Lodging House Fire', from the same collection, described by Edward Thomas as 'concentrated and shapely and powerful', the language is vital rather than poetic, as fits the theme of down-and-out existence:

> So goes my life each day—
> Its hours are twenty-four—
> Four hours I live lukewarm,
> And kill a score.

Some years later Davies wrote a poem about a dying prostitute, 'The Bird of Paradise', a daring subject at the time; yet however realistic his subject matter might be, he was never offensive, unlike John Masefield whose use of the word 'bloody' caused outrage in 1911.

Davies's second book of poems, *New Poems*, appeared in 1907 and established him as one of a new generation of poets. The same year saw the publication of collections by Gordon Bottomley, Ralph Hodgson, James Elroy Flecker, W. W. Gibson, Ford Madox Hueffer, Alfred Noyes, and James Joyce.

In December 1912 an anthology, *Georgian Poetry 1911–1912*, was published by Harold Monro's Poetry Bookshop. It was edited by Edward Marsh, dedicated to Robert Bridges, and included a rhetorical prefatorial note: 'This volume is issued in the belief that English poetry is once again putting on a new strength and beauty.' Poems were included by Lascelles Abercrombie, Gordon Bottomley, Rupert Brooke, W. H. Davies, Walter de la Mare, James Elroy Flecker, W. W. Gibson, D. H. Lawrence, John

Masefield, Harold Monro, and seven others. The title referred to the new monarch, King George V, and unintentionally gave the label of 'Georgian' to the diverse poets grouped together in this and the four anthologies which followed it.

Georgian Poetry 1911–1912 was a success. By January 1914 the book was in its ninth printing and sales eventually reached 15,000, earning the contributors good royalties. Davies wrote appreciatively to Marsh in 1916, 'You have performed a wonder, made poetry pay!' Poems by Davies were published in each of the five Georgian collections, making his work known to a readership that extended far beyond the few purchasers of new slim volumes.

In April 1914, Harold Monro published the British edition of *Des Imagistes*, extending the audience of another group of poets, the Imagists, who—unlike the Georgians—had chosen their collective name. *Des Imagistes* included poems by, among others, Richard Aldington, F. S. Flint, William Carlos Williams, James Joyce, and Ezra Pound. The Georgian poets had a much wider appeal than the more experimental Imagist poets and their commercial success proved that new poetry was enjoying widespread popularity. However, the Great War of 1914–1918 changed all this; *Georgian Poetry 1920–1922*, the fifth and last in the series, was unsuccessfully launched on an indifferent public in 1922, the year that saw the publication of T. S. Eliot's *The Waste Land* and James Joyce's *Ulysses*, two masterpieces of the modernist movement which, to some extent, had its roots in Imagism. These works meant nothing to the majority of readers who had enjoyed Georgian poetry, leaving them perplexed by the demands they made on their concentration and confused by the experimental forms in which they were written. Throughout the twenties and thirties the interest in modernist literature increased, leaving a much reduced audience for the Georgian poets—the remnants of a formerly wide non-specialist poetry reading public.

With the growing popularity of the English Literature degree course at universities, the modernist writers have attracted vast and well-deserved critical attention. But little serious work has been done on the Georgian poets as a group or individually and it is to contemporaries of Davies that one must first turn for critical appraisal of his poems.

The first and arguably still the best critic of Davies's poems was that 'wondrous necessary man' Edward Thomas, who was to become a friend of the poet. Thomas's review of *The Soul's Destroyer and Other Poems*, printed in the *Daily Chronicle*, began:

Mr William Davies is a Monmouthshire man. He has been active and passionate. He has been poor and careless and hungry and in pain . . . his 'Lodging House Fire' . . . is as simple as a caveman's drawing on bone, and yet of an atmosphere dense with old sorrow.

Thomas, in a review of *Farewell to Poesy*, printed in the *Morning Post*, also defined the main influences on Davies's poetry:

It is simple in vocabulary and rhythm and thought, and it is without conscious art; and yet the forms, the occasional conceits, and certain turns of expression make it clear that it owes much to the Elizabethan, Jacobean, and Caroline lyric as well as to Wordsworth and Blake.

Ezra Pound, a poet concerned like Davies with breaking out of a stylistic strait-jacket inherited from the nineteenth century, reviewed the *Collected Poems: First Series* for *Poetry* in 1917. He was critical of what he called Davies's 'ancient speech', but praised 'Dreams of the Sea':

This verse is not in the latest mode, but compare it with verse of its own kind and you will not find much to surpass it. Wordsworth, for instance, would have had a deal of trouble trying to better it. The sound quality is, again, nearer that of the Elizabethans than of the nineteenth-century writers . . . There is a resonance and a body of sound in these verses of Davies which I think many vers-librists might envy.

High approbation from a man so firmly placed in the modernist camp!

Charles Williams in *Poetry at Present* (Oxford University Press, 1930) included an essay which mentioned 'a wild and violent life' existing in Wordsworth and Davies, and added, 'it is only the careless reader who supposes that they are indolently contented'. Williams also noted:

And he has, it must be admitted, given us more to be surprised at; he has communicated his wonder rather than indoctrinated us with the gospel. The very nature of his verse does it; as he with the sheep, so we with his poems can only stand and stare.

Thomas Moult's *W. H. Davies* (Thornton Butterworth, 1934) combined literary criticism with personal reminiscence:

'The starlings chuckling over stolen fruit' he quotes, resuming our easy, musing talk; and, stooping, gathers some of the scattered fruit . . . 'They pock the face of all my golden pears . . . Those two lines are an example of how a thought shapes itself when it first comes to me,' he continued. 'It came like that as we walked here yesterday, and it may lead to a complete lyric when you have gone back to London. You ask me how I write. Well, there you are! I wait for a thought, an idea. I never make any attempt to write until it comes to me—I simply go on with this quiet country life, content to wait, knowing for certain that it will come sooner or later.'

The lines can be found reworked in 'Starlings': evidence that, far from being a spontaneous writer, Davies was a conscious artist and craftsman.

An essay by Davies's friend Richard Church in *Eight for Immortality* (Dent, 1941) also included literary criticism and personal reminiscence. Church commented on the often extremely generalized nature of Davies's imagery, comparing it with Tennyson's highly specific natural imagery. He valued Davies's 'fine, clear rage as lucid as his delight, as free as his joy'; 'A few tramps, a few hungry old beggar women, a cheated prostitute, a brutally used child, a tortured animal; these are the material with which Davies feeds his divine rage . . .'

Osbert Sitwell's *Noble Essences* (Little Brown & Co., 1950) is essential reading for anyone interested in Davies, 'this extraordinary and memorable being, who, for all his humility, bore about him something of the primitive splendor and directness of the Elizabethan age; in which, as his appearance testified, he would have been equally at home.' Osbert Sitwell also remarked on Davies's physical strength; despite his wooden leg he would always walk from Bloomsbury to Chelsea when visiting, rather than use transport.

More recent critical studies of Georgian poetry in general either neglect Davies or deal dismissively with his work. Robert H. Ross in his otherwise excellent *The Georgian Revolt: Rise and Fall of a Poetic Ideal 1910–22* (Faber, 1967) fails to grasp the variety and continuity to be found in Davies's poetry. He suggests that there is a division between the pre-war Davies who 'had the rare gift of spontaneity', and the post-war Davies, in whom 'spontaneity faltered, his imagination flagged. The early-morning freshness had departed.' Ross groups the poems into the early lyrics 'insistent upon the joys of nature', and the later poems of a 'pessimistic temper', whereas both are to be found throughout Davies's work.

Some of the most perceptive comments on Davies's poems are those of James Reeves. In his *A Short History of English Poetry 1340–1940* (Heinemann, 1961) he writes:

His abundant brief and simple lyrics were for many years his only source of income, and he had a certain knowing instinct for what the public wanted. Nevertheless, he was not as simple as his readers liked to think him, and as the anthologists liked to make him out. This misrepresentation has served his later reputation badly; a discriminating selection could show him for what he was—a genuine poet who combined tender and delicate feeling with a certain realistic humour and wiry homeliness.

In his anthology *Georgian Poetry* (Penguin, 1962), Reeves argues:

If any reader, anxious for technical novelty, looks at the poems of Davies and says, 'Yes, but it has been done before,' I can only answer, 'Read "The Hospital Waiting-Room" or "The Tugged Hand", and tell me by whom.' To be new, a feeling does not necessarily demand radical novelty of expression.

Reeves is right, though in fact Davies is capable of considerable manipulation of form and tone as a means of expressing subtle variations of thought and feeling.

Richard J. Stonesifer in his comprehensive *W. H. Davies: a Critical Biography* (Cape, 1963) makes many accurate and perceptive comments on specific poems and his book is obviously the result of painstaking research and prolonged thought. But he unintentionally belittles Davies by the suggestion that he created a 'Disney-world' in his poems. Stonesifer discusses Davies's poetry under the headings: 'The Humanitarian Poet', 'The Poet of Love', and 'The Poet of Nature'. Philip Larkin, in a review of Stonesifer's biography, (reprinted in *Required Writing: Miscellaneous Pieces 1955–1982*, (Faber & Faber, 1983)), suggests a further heading, 'Davies the Ironist'. Elsewhere in the same review, Larkin remarks on Davies's

knack of suddenly unearthing, as it were, some hitherto unnoticed detail or irony or pleasure and extending it for our enjoyment on the end of a far-fetched metaphor or simile. The wind dragging the corn by her long hair into the dark wood, the sheep that walk up the hill and become clouds, the wet tombstones breathing in the sun, the summer spreading a green tent on the bare pole of a tree: Davies never lost the power to refresh the commonest experience.

The point is of special relevance now that startling visual metaphor is so much in evidence in contemporary poetry. In addition to images noted by Larkin, the reader will find in the present selection: 'Crows, like merchants dressed in black,/Go leisurely to work and back,' bees that either 'roar like midget bulls' or 'Sit on their soft, fat, velvet bums,/To wriggle out of hollow flowers' and 'Those dewy cemeteries, the fields—/When they are white with mushroom tombs.'

In 'The Song of Life' Davies shows that he was well aware of the criticisms that were made against his poems by the post-war critics:

> I hear men say: 'This Davies has no depth,
> He writes of birds, of staring cows and sheep,
> And throws no light on deep, eternal things'—
> And would they have me talking in my sleep?

It is certainly true that Davies at times created an idealized natural world, but his poems on the slums, referred to earlier, and his vivid pictures of the urban life of the very poor to be found in other poems, show how misleading this criticism was. It might be added that Davies's descriptions of the countryside were not always idyllic, 'The Truth' gives a harsh account of survival in the wild, reminiscent of Thomas Hardy; 'The Rat' conveys a savagely macabre view of nature.

If further evidence is needed of Davies's range of subject matter, there are the poems about himself which express—with characteristic detachment—his knowledge and acceptance of a darker side to his own nature:

> One hour in every hundred hours
> I sing of childhood, birds and flowers;
> Who reads my character in song
> Will not see much in me that's wrong.
>
> But in my ninety hours and nine
> I would not tell what thoughts are mine:
> They're not so pure as find their words
> In songs of childhood, flowers and birds.

'Thunderstorms', another personal poem, describes Davies's inner landscape:

> My mind has thunderstorms,
>   That brood for heavy hours:
> Until they rain me words,
>   My thoughts are drooping flowers
> And sulking, silent birds.
>
> Yet come, dark thunderstorms,
>   And brood your heavy hours;
> For when you rain me words,
>   My thoughts are dancing flowers
> And joyful singing birds.

Here the tone is calm, precise, measured. There is no suggestion that the poet is indulging an emotion for rhetorical effect. The language is carefully chosen to give shape to the subject. The final rhyme word of each line is repeated in both stanzas. The first stanza expresses the mood through the metaphor of the thunderstorm, while the second stanza comments on the first in the manner of the final sestet of a sonnet. Davies is unconsciously introducing what T. S. Eliot called an 'objective correlative', taken here from phenomenological nature which provides him with the formula of a particular emotion, much as Robert Frost expressed inner feeling through the metaphor of outer weather in 'Tree at my Window'.

Davies's favoured verse form was undoubtedly the lyric written in traditional four line iambic trimeter, tetrameter, and pentameter, but in addition one finds a variety of stanza forms, songs, ballads, epigrams, blank verse, and rhyming couplets varying his collections. Many of Davies's best poems are in couplets; their manner is at once formal yet personal, their tone by turns astringent, grimly realistic, and humorous. Here is Davies at his best, within the gentle constraint of a classical form:

> Sweet Stay-at-Home, sweet Well-content,
> Thou knowest of no strange continent:
> Thou hast not felt they bosom keep
> A gentle motion with the deep;

'The Sea' contains a scene of dramatic power conveyed in language of stark simplicity:

> I saw that woman go from place
> To place, hungry for her child's face;
> I heard her crying, crying, crying;
> Then, in a flash! saw the Sea trying,
> With savage joy, and efforts wild,
> To smash his rocks with a dead child.

In marked contrast Davies wrote a considerable number of poems which fit the standard definition of 'Georgian'; that is to say, poems with a rural setting expressing pleasure in country life. Such poems as 'The Kingfisher' or 'The Moon' were popular features of the Georgian poetry anthologies, but it must be remembered that the same anthologies contained Davies's realist poems as well. Whatever the contemporary reader makes of the famous 'songs of childhood, flowers and birds', these can now be seen as forming only one part of a body of work surprisingly varied in form and theme.

Commenting on the Augustus John portrait of Davies done in 1918, (and reproduced on the cover of this collection), Richard Church wrote in *The Voyage Home* (Heinemann, 1964): 'It sums up the cunning peasant-like quiddities of character which directed Davies's reactions to events and people. He would have been less original without them.' Osbert Sitwell observed a 'certain shrewdness' in Davies, combined with his simplicity of nature. It is thanks to this complexity of character that there is such variety within the work.

Davies's strength lies in his fidelity to personal experience, his wholehearted embrace of what life offers, be it enjoyable or not, and an unshowy but nonetheless effective literary artistry. These qualities are apparent throughout his work, when read selectively, from 'The Lodging House Fire' of 1905 to the visionary title poem of his last collection *The Loneliest Mountain and Other Poems* of 1939, the language of which in its own quiet way is as concrete as that of any poetry of the time:

> The loneliest mountain, with no house or tree,
>   Still has its little flower so sweet and wild;
> While I, a dreamer, strange and but half known,
>   Can find no equal till I meet a child.

Perhaps what one values above all in the work of W. H. Davies, are those same qualities which he found so admirable in Robert Burns: '. . . his candour and sincerity. He was not ashamed to mention anything that gave him pleasure, whether it was love or ale; and he was too truthful and sincere to hide anything that made him grieve.'

A CHRONOLOGY OF
W. H. DAVIES'S LIFE AND WORK

APART from information from Davies's own autobiographies, this chronology is largely based on a collation of information contained in Richard J. Stonesifer's *W. H. Davies: A Critical Biography* (Cape, 1963), Lawrence Hockey's *W. H. Davies* (University of Wales Press on behalf of the Welsh Arts Council, 1971), and the bibliography and biographical article on W. H. D. by Sybil Hollingdrake contained in the W. H. Davies special issue of *Poetry Wales*, Vol. 18, No. 2 (Poetry Wales Press, 1983) to whom thanks are due.

1871	20 April	William Henry Davies born, the second of three children, to Francis Davies, an iron-moulder, and Mary Ann Davies. *The Autobiography of a Super-Tramp* begins: 'I was born thirty-five years ago, in a public house called the Church House, in the town of N—, in the county of M—.' The Church House Inn, 14 Portland Street, Newport, Monmouthshire, on the edge of the Old Town Dock, has been queried as W. H. D.'s birth-place by Lawrence Hockey who claims that the birth certificate bears the date 3 July and that W. H. D. was born at 6 Portland Street. Mary Ann Davies was Welsh, the daughter of Gomer and Ann Evans of Newport; but Francis Davies's father, Captain Francis Boase Davies, a master mariner, came from Cornwall, and his wife Lydia Adams Davies, a strict and zealous Baptist, came from Somerset. Lydia Adams Davies was related to the actor Henry Irving; Osbert Sitwell in *Noble Essences* records that W. H. D. quotes her as describing Irving as 'that young Brodribb cousin of yours who's brought disgrace upon the family!'
1874	November	W. H. D.'s father dies aged 31. See 'R. is for Remembrance'.
1875	September	Mary Ann Davies remarries. Captain Francis Boase Davies and his wife Lydia adopt their

		three grandchildren who move to the Church House Inn.

1879   Captain Davies retires as an innkeeper. The family moves to 38 Raglan Street. See chapter 1 of *The Autobiography of a Super-Tramp*: 'When we were settled in private life our home consisted of grandfather, grandmother, an imbecile brother, a sister, myself, a maidservant, a dog, a cat, a parrot, a dove, and a canary bird.' See 'The Child and the Mariner', 'A Poet's Epitaph'.

1884   W. H. D. birched for shoplifting. At about this time reads Byron, Shelley, Marlowe, and Shakespeare, but 'indifferent to Wordsworth' —his grandmother suggesting instead Milton and Young.

1885   W. H. D. leaves Alexandra Road Boys' School, aged 14, and works for an ironmonger. Lydia encourages him to attend Sunday school at the Commercial Road Baptist Church.

1886   May   Captain Davies dies aged 76.

       November   Lydia Davies has W. H. D. apprenticed to Jeremiah Williams, a picture-framer and gilder. At about this time W. H. D. writes and has printed a poem describing 'a storm at night, which a young friend recited at a mutual improvement class'. Attends the theatre and presents an 'article to the same class entitled "In defence of the Stage" '. See *The Autobiography of a Super-Tramp*, chapter 2, where W. H. D. also writes, 'I was now bound apprentice to the picture frame trade, but owing to my passion for reading, could not apply myself sufficiently to that business so as to become a good workman.'

1888   At about this time W. H. D. encouraged by an intelligent young woman from a nearby village, before her tragically early death. 'Her encouragement at that early time has been the star on which these eyes have seldom closed, by which I have successfully navigated the deeps of misery, pushing aside Drink, my first officer, who many a day and many a night endeavoured to founder me.' *The Autobiography of a Super-Tramp*, chapter 2.

1891		W. H. D. completes his apprenticeship. About this time visits London, 'walking the streets at night', discovering, what he called in *Beggars*, 'five weeks' experience of the worst side of life'. Finds work in Bristol with a picture-frame maker. In *The Autobiography of a Super-Tramp*, chapter 2, writes of this period, 'The licence indulged in during these six months, being in a strange town and unknown, was sufficient to wreck the brains and health of any man beyond recovery, and for the time being deadened all literary ambition.'
1893	March	W. H. D.'s grandmother dies. W. H. D. returns to Newport to find her estate left in trust with an executor, Jacob Waite, who divides the profits weekly among the three grandchildren, thereby ensuring W. H. D. of a weekly income of ten shillings. W. H. D. soon obtains an advance from the trustee and 'full of hope and expectation' at the age of 22 sets sails for America from Liverpool in June. Here begin W. H. D.'s six years of tramping back and forth over America, sometimes in the company of drifters such as Brum and Australian Red, sometimes alone. He jumps free train rides, winters in gaols or at the port of Baltimore, spends the summers travelling and intermittently working at fruit- or hop-picking, or labouring. These years are vividly recreated in *The Autobiography of a Super-Tramp*.
1894		Trip back to England working on a cattle-ship—the first of many such working passages back and forth across the Atlantic, sometimes on ships carrying sheep as well as cattle. See 'Sheep' and 'A Child's Pet'. W. H. D. sickened by the cruelty shown towards the animals by the cattle-men.
1898		An appreciative newspaper article on the work of Robert Burns reminds W. H. D. of his early literary ambitions and he returns first to Newport, then to London, but cannot settle. By the

following year has returned to America to join in the Klondike Gold Rush.

1899	March	In Renfrew, Ontario, W. H. D.'s right foot is severed at the ankle when jumping a moving train, leading to amputation of his right leg above the knee. After the accident, while waiting for a doctor to arrive in the nearby station waiting-room, 'I could see no other way of keeping a calm face before such a number of eyes than by taking out my pipe and smoking, an action which, I am told, caused much sensation in the local press.' *The Autobiography of a Super-Tramp*, chapter 19.
	June	W. H. D. returns to Newport where, at night, he teaches himself to walk with an artificial limb. 'I was now more content with my lot, determined that as my body had failed, my brains should now have the chance they had longed for, when the spirit had been bullied into submission by the body's activity.' *The Autobiography of a Super-Tramp*, chapter 21.
	August	To London, determined to live prudently on his dwindling legacy, now 8s. a week (2s. went to his family in Newport), and to devote himself to literature. Moves to lodgings in Rowton House in Newington Butts (and stays for two years); writes 'The Robber', a blank verse tragedy, and over 100 sonnets, all rejected for publication.
1900		At about this time W. H. D. privately prints three or four poems on a single sheet of paper in the hope of selling 2,000 copies from door to door. This plan fails and he burns the sheets in disgust.
1901		Moves to The Ark Salvation Army hostel in Southwark.
1902	September	Leaves The Ark with a wooden peg leg, as a licensed pedlar, but his wares (pins, needles, and buttons) are ruined by damp and, after Christmas, he returns to London. At about this time sees a man reading in a Lambeth doss-house; years later W. H. D. realizes this was Francis Thompson. See 'Francis Thompson'.

1903		At about this time W. H. D. moves to The Farmhouse, a superior hostel in Marshalsea Road, Southwark. See 'The Lodging House Fire'.
1904	May	Submits manuscript of *The Soul's Destroyer and Other Poems* to Watts & Co., who request £19 for publication.
	July	W. H. D. forgoes all income from his legacy, now six shillings, for some time in an agreement with Jacob Waite to save the necessary sum for publication of the book. W. H. D. tramps around the country for five to six months.
1905		Collects copies of *The Soul's Destroyer and Other Poems* from the printer. The book contains 40 poems printed in an edition of 250, priced at 2s. 6d. Eventually sends copies to potential purchasers selected from *Who's Who* in the hope that the price will be refunded. Receives replies from St. John Adcock, Arthur Symons, and George Bernard Shaw, who sends money for additional copies 'to send them to such critics and verse fanciers as he knew of, wondering whether they would recognise a poet when they met one'. Preface by George Bernard Shaw to *The Autobiography of a Super-Tramp*. W. H. D. is featured as a tramp poet in newspaper articles. Callers visit The Farmhouse in search of him.
	October	Edward Thomas visits W. H. D. and reviews *The Soul's Destroyer and Other Poems* in the *Daily Chronicle*. W. H. D. plans a second volume of poems. Moves back to Newport to be with his family, but by the end of the year is forced to leave a pleasant house in Woodland Road by the landlady. Plans his autobiography.
	November	Begins work on his autobiography. The narrative of *The Autobiography of a Super-Tramp* ends at this point.
	December	Visited at Newport by Edward Thomas who invites W. H. D. to share his small study-cottage in Kent.
1906	February	W. H. D. moves to Stidulph's Cottage, Egg Pie Lane, The Weald, near Sevenoaks, Kent, rented

for him by Edward Thomas who lives a few miles away at Elses Farm with his family. Thomas obtains books and collects enough money for the village wheelwright to make a new leg for W. H. D. Thomas soon introduces W. H. D. to Edward Garnett who also lives nearby; and then, on Tuesday trips to London, introduces him to the midday literary gathering held at the Mont Blanc, Gerrard Street, Soho. W. H. D. meets, among others, Walter de la Mare, Norman Douglas, Joseph Conrad, H. M. Tomlinson, John Masefield, Hilaire Belloc, and W. H. Hudson. Tea at the St. George Restaurant in St. Martin's Lane often follows lunch; *habitués* include Gordon Bottomley, Walter de la Mare, and Ralph Hodgson and his dog. 'Hodgson was a man to my own mind, for we both preferred to talk of dogs and prize-fighters instead of poets and poetry.' *Later Days*, chapter five.

	December	The Thomases move to Ashford, Petersfield. W. H. D. rewriting the autobiography. Continues to visit the Mont Blanc and St. George Restaurant on day trips to London.
1907	January	*New Poems* (Elkin Mathews). W. H. D.'s second book of poems.
	March	Second edition of *The Soul's Destroyer and Other Poems* (Alston Rivers). This revised edition contains only 14 of the original 40 poems.
1908	April	*The Autobiography of a Super-Tramp* (Fifield) with a preface by George Bernard Shaw (who also suggested the title), Thomas finding the publisher. Mrs Shaw contributes to cost of production.
	October	*Nature Poems and Others* (Fifield).
1909	July	W. H. D. moves to lodgings in Sevenoaks, Kent.
	September	*Beggars* (Duckworth). A prose work.
1910	March	*Farewell to Poesy and Other Pieces* (Fifield). Various poems in the book had already appeared in the *Nation*. From now on W. H. D. submits poems to a variety of periodicals before book publication.
1911	February	*A Weak Woman* (Duckworth). W. H. D.'s first

novel. With the aid of Prime Minister Asquith, Edward Thomas and Edward Garnett arrange a petition which secures W. H. D. a Civil List pension of £50 a year. They had previously arranged a small sinecure at the British Museum which W. H. D. turned down, not wanting to be tied to a job.

April	Edward Garnett also secures W. H. D. financial help from the Royal Literary Fund.
November	*Songs of Joy and Others* (Fifield).
December	W. H. D. spends his customary Christmas with the Thomases in Petersfield.

1912 March *The True Traveller* (Duckworth). Prose pieces. Sybil Hollingdrake has written of the 'honesty and compassion' of W. H. D.'s descriptions in this book of his experience of prostitutes during his travels.

December *Georgian Poetry 1911–1912* (Poetry Bookshop). Edited by Edward Marsh (although his name does not appear on the title page). This extremely influential anthology includes five poems by W. H. D. together with work by sixteen other poets, including Rupert Brooke, G. K. Chesterton, Walter de la Mare, W. W. Gibson, D. H. Lawrence, and Harold Monro. The success of the anthology leads to four others, each of which contains poems by W. H. D. Sales of the first volume alone eventually total 15,000, making the contributors a reasonable sum from royalties.

1913 January Opening of the Poetry Bookshop, 35 Devonshire Street, Theobalds Road, London. W. H. D. attends the opening, as do Henry Newbolt, Edward Marsh, F. S. Flint, Robert Frost, and many others including, of course, the proprietor Harold Monro. W. H. D. often visits the Poetry Bookshop on trips to London.

July W. H. D. meets D. H. Lawrence.
September *Foliage: Various Poems* (Elkin Mathews).

1914 January At about this time W. H. D. returns to London. Meets George Bernard Shaw, Alice Meynell, Rupert Brooke, Conrad Aiken, and John Freeman.

	March	*Nature: Selections from the Prose and Poetry of W. H. Davies* (Batsford). Edited by Mary Stratton.
	November	*The Bird of Paradise and Other Poems* (Methuen).
1915	November	*Georgian Poetry 1913–1915* (Poetry Bookshop). Includes nine poems by W. H. D. W. H. D.'s Civil List pension increased to £100, probably through the efforts of Harold Monro and Edward Marsh.
1916		W. H. D. moves into two rooms over a shop at 14 Great Russell Street where he stays for six years, despite rats and difficult neighbours.
	June	*Child Lovers and Other Poems* (Fifield).
	November	*Collected Poems: First Series* (Fifield). With a frontispiece from a pencil sketch of W. H. D. by William Rothenstein and a facsimile note in W. H. D.'s handwriting; a selection of 111 numbered poems arranged non-chronologically. Knopf publish the American edition. At about this time, during the latter War years, W. H. D. meets a number of painters and other artists: Henri Gaudier-Brzeska, Jacob Epstein, Harold Gilman, Augustus John, Nina Hamnett, Harold and Laura Knight, William Nicholson, William Rothenstein, and Walter Sickert. W. H. D. begins to assemble a collection of portraits of himself. Also in the latter War years W. H. D. reads at poetry recitals, together with other contemporary poets, to help the War effort, and becomes a celebrated reader of his own work. Possibly as a result of this W. H. D. receives invitations from Lady Asquith, Lady Ritchie, Lady Cunard, and Lady Churchill.
1917	April	Edward Thomas killed at Arras. Thomas described by W. H. D. as 'my first and oldest literary friend'. See 'Killed in Action'.
	November	*Georgian Poetry 1916–1917* (Poetry Bookshop). Includes four poems by W. H. D.
1918		At about this time meets Osbert and Sacheverell Sitwell who introduce him to Edith Sitwell, Robert Nichols, and Aldous Huxley. Also

		meets Richard Church; tells him, 'Never lose your enthusiasm.'
	March	*A Poet's Pilgrimage* (Melrose). A prose book incorporating material gathered from a number of walking tours over the years. The book incorporates new poems in the text, mostly at the head of chapters.
	May	*Raptures: a Book of Poems* (Beaumont Press). Edition of 272 copies.
		New Palls: an Anthology of Poems Dedicated to the Memory of Rupert Brooke. Contains two poems by W. H. D.
	October	*Forty New Poems* (Fifield). Reprints 30 poems from *Raptures* and includes 12 new poems.
1919		At about this time meets Martin Armstrong and Arnold Bennett.
	November	*Georgian Poetry 1918–1919* (Poetry Bookshop). Includes eight poems by W. H. D.
1920	September	*The Song of Life and Other Poems* (Fifield). With a frontispiece of W. H. D. by Laura Knight. Increase in Civil List pension to £150 a year.
1921	September	*The Captive Lion and Other Poems* (Yale University Press). Contains *Forty New Poems* and *The Song of Life*. Published in the U.S.A.
	October	First issue of *Form*, a monthly magazine which runs for only four issues and of which W. H. D. is literary editor and co-editor with Austin O. Spare.
		At about this time A. C. Fifield retires and Jonathan Cape takes over as W. H. D.'s publisher, reissuing his early books in cheaply priced editions. By the end of the year moves to better accommodation at 13 Avery Row, Brook Street.
1922		Throughout this year W. H. D. seriously ill with what he refers to in *Later Days* as 'rheumatism and fever' but also calls in *Young Emma* a venereal infection. At about this time meets Helen Matilda Payne, a country girl in her early twenties. The realistic and moving story of their love is told in *Young Emma* (Cape, 1980).
	January	Final issue of *Form*.

	September	*The Hour of Magic and Other Poems* (Cape). With decorations by William Nicholson.
	October	*Shorter Lyrics of the Twentieth Century: 1900–1922* (Poetry Bookshop). An anthology selected with a foreword by W. H. D.
	November	*Georgian Poetry 1920–1922* (Poetry Bookshop). Includes six poems by W. H. D. At the end of the year W. H. D. and Helen move to East Grinstead, Sussex.
1923	February	W. H. D. and Helen marry at the Registry Office, East Grinstead, with Martin Armstrong and Conrad Aiken as witnesses. The narrative of *Later Days* concludes at the end of this year, ending with a memorable picture of the couple's home life with a pet cat and dog. W. H. D. attempts, unsuccessfully, to persuade Clifford Bax to collaborate with him on his tramp opera *True Travellers*.
	April	*Collected Poems: Second Series* (Cape). With a portrait in oils by Augustus John. 112 poems arranged non-chronologically, selected from *New Poems, Foliage, Forty New Poems, The Song of Life* and *The Hour of Magic*. *Selected Poems* (Cape) decorated with woodcuts by Stephen Bone.
	October	*True Travellers: A Tramp's Opera in Three Acts* (Cape). With illustrations by William Nicholson. This play includes lyrics and has never been staged, but the book itself is one of the most attractive of all W. H. D.'s volumes.
1924	April	*Secrets* (Cape). With occasional unacknowledged decorations. *Moll Flanders* by Daniel Defoe (Simpkin, Marshall, Hamilton, Kent & Co.). With biographical note and introduction by W. H. D.
	August	W. H. D. writing *Young Emma*, which he sends to Jonathan Cape six weeks later.
	November	George Bernard Shaw advises Cape against publication of *Young Emma* (the letter is included as an appendix to the 1980 edition). Nonetheless, Shaw calls the book 'an amazing document'. Meanwhile W. H. D. requests that the original MS be destroyed, and instead com-

mences work on *Later Days* where the story is told in chapters 13 and 14.

1925		*Burns' Poetical Works* (Collins' Clear-Type Press). With introduction by W. J. Davies (sic). Probably published this year.
	October	*Later Days* (Cape). A sequel to *The Autobiography of a Super-Tramp*. Poems included in the text.
	November	*A Poet's Alphabet* (Cape). With decorations by Dora M. Batty. *Augustan Books of Modern Poetry: W. H. Davies* (Benn). Includes 30 selected poems.
1926	July	University of Wales awards W. H. D. the degree of Doctor in Litteris, *honoris causa* (which he receives in 1929).
	October	*The Song of Love* (Cape). With decorations by Dora M. Batty. A sequence of 100 numbered quatrains. *The Adventures of Johnny Walker, Tramp* (Cape); foreword: 'I have used the experiences selected in *Beggars* and *The True Traveller* but I have . . . made the book run as a story . . . with some new material added.'
1927	October	*A Poet's Calendar* (Cape).
	November	*Dancing Mad* (Cape). W. H. D.'s second novel.
1928	October	*The Collected Poems of W. H. Davies, 1928* (Cape). With frontispiece photograph of bust by Jacob Epstein: a collection of 431 poems with an introductory note by W. H. D. *Selected Poems*, arranged by Edward Garnett, with a foreword by W. H. D., and frontispiece by Augustus John (Gregynog Press). 310 copies.
	November	*Forty-Nine Poems* (Medici Society). Selected and illustrated by Jacynth Parsons, with a preface by W. H. D. *Moss and Feather* (Faber & Gwyer). A poem in the *Ariel* series with illustration by William Nicholson.
1929	October	*Ambition and other Poems* (Cape). At about this time the Davieses move to the Cotswold town of Nailsworth, Gloucestershire. (Previous addresses since East Grinstead include Sevenoaks and Malpus House, Oxted.) Over the next ten years they move from one Nailsworth house to another: Shenstone, The

Croft, Yewdales, and Glendower. W. H. D.'s friends now include William Rothenstein, Brian Waters, Thomas Moult, John Haines, and Mrs Gordon Woodhouse; but from now on W. H. D. lives in pleasant semi-retirement, fulfilling some of the early ambitions expressed in the poem 'Truly great'. See also 'Taking Stock' and poems from *My Garden* and *My Birds*. Visits Newport from time to time and is visited at Nailsworth by his nephew Noel Phillips.

1930		Newport holds a civic lunch in honour of W. H. D.
	September	*Jewels of Song: an Anthology of Short Poems* (Cape). Compiled and with an introduction by W. H. D.
1931	September	*In Winter: A Poem* (privately printed for Fytton Armstrong). With decoration by Edward Carrick. 305 copies.
1932	October	*Poems 1930–31* (Cape). Decorated by Elizabeth Montgomery.
1933	March	*My Birds* (Cape). Decorated by Hilda M. Quick. Essays on birds seen in W. H. D.'s garden. *My Garden* (Cape). Decorated by Hilda M. Quick. Both books include poems as well as prose essays.
	November	*The Lovers' Song-Book* (Gregynog Press). 30 poems in an edition of 250 copies.
1934	September	*The Poems of W. H. Davies* (Cape). The 431 poems from the volume of 1928 with the addition of poems from *Ambition, Poems 1930–31, My Birds*, and *My Garden*.
	November	*The English Country* (Wishart). Edited by H. J. Massingham, with a chapter on the Cotswolds by W. H. D.
1935	April	*Love Poems* (Cape). Includes *The Lovers' Song-Book* and 20 additional poems.
1936	October	*The Birth of Song: Poems 1935–36* (Cape). With unacknowledged decorations.
1938	May	Reissue of *Jewels of Song* under the title *Anthology of Short Poems* (Cape).
	September	A plaque placed on the Church House Inn, Newport: 'Wm. Henry Davies/poet & author/born here/1871'. W. H. D.'s last public

appearance. John Masefield speaks at the ceremony.

1939	October	*The Loneliest Mountain and Other Poems* (Cape). Includes a note by W. H. D: 'My doctor advises that the only hope of prolonging my life is to become lazy and selfish. If I live another year or two, there may be a small Scrapbook, consisting of poems ... But, whatever happens, the present book ends my career as a living author.'
1940	April	*The Poems of W. H. Davies, 1940* (Cape). With a portrait by Laura Knight. The 533 poems from the volume of 1934 with the addition of poems from *Love Poems*, *The Birth of Song*, and *The Loneliest Mountain*. About this time W. H. D. tells his friend Brian Waters, 'I've done what I set out to do.'
	September	W. H. D. dies at his home, Glendower, Nailsworth.
1941	April	*Common Joys and Other Poems* (Faber). A selection of 62 poems in the *Sesame Books* series.
1942		*Collected Poems of W. H. Davies* (Cape). With the portrait from the 1940 edition, acknowledged by Harold Knight, and containing the same poems as the volume of 1940.
1943		*Collected Poems of W. H. Davies* (Cape). Second impression includes an introduction by Osbert Sitwell, otherwise identical to the 1942 volume.
1951	April	*The Essential W. H. Davies* (Cape). Selected with an introduction by Brian Waters. Contains both prose and poetry.
1963		*The Complete Poems of W. H. Davies* (Cape). With an introduction by Osbert Sitwell and a foreword by Daniel George. Daniel George adds to the 636 poems first gathered together in 1940 a further 113 poems included in W. H. D.'s individual books but omitted from the 1940 volume. Published simultaneously with *W. H. Davies: a Critical Biography* by Richard J. Stonesifer (Cape).
1971		*W. H. Davies* by Lawrence Hockey (University of Wales Press on behalf of the Welsh Arts

Council). A biographical and bibliographical study in the *Writers of Wales* series.

1979   Mrs Helen Matilda Davies dies.

1980   *Young Emma* (Cape). Published for the first time; with a foreword by C. V. Wedgwood.

1983   *Poetry Wales* (Poetry Wales Press). W. H. Davies special issue, Vol. 18, No. 2. Edited by Cary Archard and Sandra Anstey with articles by Sybil Hollingdrake, Jonathan Barker, R. George Thomas, Fiona Pearson, and Lawrence W. Hockey, as well as poems, photographs, chronology, and a bibliography by Sybil Hollingdrake.

A NOTE ON THE SELECTION

THE 20 individual volumes of new poems and other books containing poems published during Davies's lifetime include just under 800 poems. A number of these books, and one special edition, were published in the U.S.A. In addition, four selections from published work and five volumes of collected poems were issued in Davies's lifetime. Since then one selection, *Common Joys and Other Poems* (Faber), was published in 1941; one anthology of the poems and prose, *The Essential W. H. Davies*, edited by Brian Waters (Cape), was published in 1951; and one volume of *The Complete Poems of W. H. Davies* (Cape), with an introduction by Osbert Sitwell and a foreword by Daniel George, was published in 1963. Of the volumes of collected poems, the first, *Collected Poems: First Series* (Fifield), was published in 1916 and included a non-chronological selection of 111 numbered poems including three previously unpublished ones, and a facsimile note in the author's handwriting: 'This single volume collection of what I believe to be my best pieces is published in response to a frequently expressed wish from the press and the public . . .' A second volume, *Collected Poems: Second Series* (Cape), appeared in 1923, with a further non-chronological selection of 112 numbered poems. *The Collected Poems of W. H. Davies, 1928*, was published by Cape in that year. This was the first chronologically numbered edition and included 431 poems. Davies contributed an introductory note: 'In this one volume are collected all the poems I care to remember, and a number of others that I would like to forget; written from the beginning of my career in 1905, right up to the present year of 1928. It is a question of public demand, as people prefer an author as he is, at his worst as well as at his best. But the author has this consolation: no two readers will agree as to which are his best poems and which are his worst.' In 1934 came *The Poems of W. H. Davies* (Cape), which included 533 numbered poems. *The Poems of W. H. Davies, 1940* (Cape) included 636 numbered poems. This volume was reprinted in 1942 after the poet's death as *Collected Poems of W. H. Davies*; the second impression of 1943 included an introduction by Osbert Sitwell. *The Complete Poems of W. H. Davies* (Cape) was published in 1963 with Osbert Sitwell's introduction and a foreword by Daniel George, who added 113 poems from individual volumes which had been excluded from one or other of the previous collected editions. These 113 poems were, confusingly, added to the 636 of 1940 as numbers 637–749 at the end of the book—a fact not acknowledged in the text. On further examination it became clear that the apparently chronological arrangement adopted from 1928 diverged in a number of places from the order of first book publication.

In making this selection I have taken the opportunity to return to the strict chronological order of first book publication, except in the case of *Raptures* (1918) and *The Lovers' Song-Book* (1933), both reprinted with additional poems as *Forty New Poems* (1918) and *Love Poems* (1935) respectively—when the order of the later has been adopted. The text of each poem has been checked against that of the first publication in book form. Literal printing errors, insignificant respellings, and minor amendments to punctuation, have been silently corrected to conform to the texts of the 1928, 1934, and 1940 volumes which were published during Davies's lifetime and therefore incorporate what we must assume is his final text. Any interesting variation on the final text in the first publication of a poem is indicated in the footnotes.

Some poems which appeared in the 1905 edition of *The Soul's Destroyer and Other Poems*, but were omitted from the 1907 edition, are reprinted here for the first time, together with some short poems taken from Davies's prose books. The title of the volume in which each poem first appeared is given in the list of contents at the front of the present volume.

This is the first paperback selection of the poems and the first *Selected Poems* to appear for over forty years. Within the space available I have sought to present a selection which includes poems representing something of the entire range of Davies's work. Limitation of space has led to the editorial decision to include the longer poems in extract only. (The one exception is 'The Child and the Mariner'.) I have also preferred to do without a barrage of possibly superfluous notes on the text and have included instead as many poems as possible. My intention has been to allow this selection, amounting to over one third of the poems, to aid a proper evaluation of the achievement of this poet. At the back of my mind has been the note included by W. H. Davies in *The Song of Love* in 1926: 'In writing these verses I am attempting to make poetry popular. That is to say, I would like to give as much pleasure to the general reader as to the student of poetry. Whether I succeed or not remains to be seen.'

from The Soul's Destroyer

London! What utterance the mind finds here!
In its academy of art, more rich[1]
Than that proud temple which made Ophir poor,
And the resources famed of Sheba's Queen.
And its museums, hoarding up the past,
With their rare bones of animals extinct;
And woven stuffs embroidered by the East
Ere other hemispheres could know that Peace
Had trophies pleasanter to win than War;
The great man, wrought to very life in stone—
Of genius, that raises spirits that
It cannot lay until their will is wrought—
Till in their eyes we seek to wander awed,
Lost in the mind's immensity, to find
The passage barred, the spirit gone away.
And not without sweet sounds to hear: as I
Have heard the music, like a hiding child,
Low chuckling its delight behind a wall,
Which, with a sudden burst and joyous cry,
Out leapt and on my heart threw its sweet weight—
When strolling in the palace-bounded parks
Of our great city on a summer's morn.
Now, one who lives for long in London town
Doth feel his love divided 'tween the two—
A city's noise and Nature's quiet call:
His heart is as a mother's, that can hear
Voices of absent children o'er the sea
Calling to her, and children's words[2] at home.
E'en when old Thames rolls in his fog, and men
Are lost, and only blind men know their way;
When Morning borrows of the Evening's lamps,
Or when bewildered millions battle home
With stifled throats, and eyes that burn with[3] pain

---

[1] more rich [richer 1905, 1907]
[2] words [voices 1905, 1907]   [3] with [to 1905]

Still are there lovers faithful to such moods.
But in thy slums, where I have seen men gaunt,
In their vile prisons where they wander starved
Without a jailer for their common needs—
Heard children whimper to their mother's moan;
Where rich ones, had they love with willing hands,
Have privilege to win their godhead soon
By charity that's needless in new realms—
Oh, who can love thy slums with starving ones!
Where children live, like flowers in Ocean's dells,
Unvisited by light or balmy wind:
As daffodils, that plead with their sweet smiles[4]
Our charity for their rude father March.
Thy place is in the slums, O Charity,
These are thy churches for thy visitings;
The charity that seeks is nobler far
Than charity that must at home be sought.
This London served my life for full five years.
In sheer disgust to know intemperance
And poverty, and leaning to the sot
Who lays this precious intellect to sleep,
As though no beauty was in all the world,
With heaven and earth scarce worthy of a thought,
And helpless grown of every future joy—
Methought return to Nature might restore
Youth's early peace and faith's simplicity.
Though Hope be an illusion, yet our life
Were never so bewildered as without it;
An April day of sunny promises
When we are suffering actual cold and want,
And child of Discontent—without such hints
Of coming joy Life's name were Vanity.
Hopeless had I become, a wreck of men;
A derelict that neither sinks nor floats,
Is drifting out of sight of heaven and earth,
Not of the ways of men, but *in* their ways . . .

[4] their sweet smiles [their smiles 1905]

2

. . . One morning I awoke with lips gone dry,
The tongue an obstacle to choke the throat,
And aching body weighted with more heads
Than Pluto's dog; the features hard and set,
As though encasèd in a plaster cast;
With limbs all sore through falling here and there
To drink the various ales the Borough kept
From London Bridge to Newington, and streets
Adjoining, alleys, lanes obscure from them,
Then thought of home and of the purer life,
Of Nature's air, and having room to breathe,
A sunny sky, green field, and water's sound;
Of peaceful rivers not yet fretful grown
As when their mouths have tasted Ocean's salt;
And where the rabbits sit amid their ferns,
Or leap, to flash the white of their brown tails.
Less time a grey crow picks the partridge clean,
I was apparelled, and, with impulse that
Was wonderful in one of many sprees,
Went onward rapidly[5] from street to street.
I still had vision clear of Nature's face,
Though muddled in my senses to the ways
And doings of the days and nights before.
I heard the city roaring like a beast
That's wronged by one that feared an open strife
And triumphed by his[6] cunning—as I walked.
It followed on for hours with rushing sound,
As[7] some great cataract had burst all bounds
And was oncoming with its mingled[8] pines—
The fallen sentinels—to choke the sea.
Once in awhile the sound, though not less near,
Seemed distant, barred by dwellings closely joined,
But at a corner's turn heard full again;
Yet lessened soon and sure to softer ways

[5] Went onward rapidly [Went rapidly 1907, 1928]
[6] his [its 1905]   [7] As [Though 1905]
[8] mingled [mangled 1905, 1907]

3

Of a low murmuring—as though it found[9]
Anger was vain, and coaxed for my return.
All day walked I, and that same night, I scorned[10]
The shelter of a house, lay peaceful down
Beneath the glorious stars; beneath that nest
Of singing stars men call the Milky Way;
Thought it, maybe, the way that spirits take,
And heavenly choir to sing triumphal march
For dead men for the New Jerusalem.
I was alone: had left the Borough in
Safe care of my old cronies, who would keep
Its reputation from becoming changed
Into a quiet neighbourhood. . .

The Rill

Sweet rill, that gnawed thy way through rocks,
    And under hidden roots did crawl,
Lost, found, in dark and light, now in
    This hollow resting after all—

Though red the hills, not all their gold
    Could flatter thee with them to stay:
Thou hurried down the steps where camped
    The gorse that burned the green away.

I heard thy murmur, when afar,
    Though sweet, 'twas seeming full of care;
Such protest made of Innocence
    To flowers Beauty spurned from wear.

9 as though it found [though it had found 1905]
10 scorned [scorning 1905, 1907]

Here, all thine early struggles o'er,
  As a contented pool to rest,
Thy secrets searched by heaven's stars,
  Come new or old—they search thy breast.

Here, flowers will tend thy banks and glint,
  Birds charming thee in Summer's hours;
The spider here will walk his bridge,
  His bridge built spanning waves of flowers.

The earth's blind mole hath joints of steel,
  Swims solid earth—strong swimmer he;
And heaves his billows to earth's top,
  Which unbelieving men can see—

But thou hast made thy way through rocks,
  And under hidden roots did crawl,
And thy prosperity is in
  This hollow resting after all.

Would, after all, thy peace were mine,
  And better prospects filled my ken:
The way is dark, no light yet seen,
  My rocks they are the hearts of men.

In a Lodging House

'Get to thy room,' a voice told me,
'From sottish lips in blasphemy';
And I said this: 'If I go there,
Silence will send me to[11] Despair;
Then my weak What I Am will be
Mocked by that one I wish to be;

[11] me to [to me 1905]

5

And leeches of regret will lie
On me to palely stupefy,
Close sucking at my heart's content'—
Yet I arose, to my room went.
I knew't: scarce off my garments were
When came the funeral gathering there
To bury my dead hopes, as night
By night to mock my Fancy's sight.
There was a meeting-house adjoined,
Where rich ones, rare and few of kind,
Fed little children, came to cheer
Parents with music sweet to hear.
While now I grieved a real voice stole
Into my room, and sang this soul
To heaven from hell, though I knew well
Silence would drift it back to hell
When that sweet sound was heard no more.
She sang to me[12] a chanted shore
Where seamaids' dripping tresses spread
And made[13] the rocks gold carpeted;
She sang me back to childhood's way,
To fields with lambs to see at play,
And sheep that coughed like men. Again
I saw quaint treasures of the main,
Dried fishes, model ships, and shells,
And coral stalks, and seaweed bells,
In my grandfather's house. Ah! sweet
To bear his boast through school and street—
'Master of my own ship was I.'
Again I heard his footsteps nigh,
As to and fro the passage dark
He walked, as though on his own bark;
When granny, I, a sister, brother,
Huddled under cosy cover.
Now have I lived my score and ten,
Yet less my hope than older men.

[12] to me [me to 1905]   [13] And made [To make 1905]

No collier bowelled in the earth
But Hope shall flush with rosy breath;
No seaman drowning in the main,
Nor traveller perished on a plain,
Where all is silent, and the wind
Prowls day and night in vain to find
A living thing to make a moan,
Or mountaineer was lost—nay, none
Of these but Hope makes less afraid,
And flatters to some call for aid.
Yet here lives one a score and ten,
And less his hope than older men.
I cared not for that singer's grace,
If plain she were or fair of face,
Or what her station, age might be—
She was a Voice, no more to me,
But such an one, so sweet and fresh,
I made no judgment on her flesh.
It seemed a spirit there to float,
Alighting with such raptured note
That it must ease its heart of. Oh,
Woman; thy sweet voice none others know
As those[14] to whom thou'rt seldom heard;
Who have no flower to tend, no bird
For pet, no child to play—to give
A cultured joy to ones that live
In common lodging house. To hear
A sweet voice is to me more dear
Than sound of organs, bands, or bells.
Discordant bursts lead out soft swells
Of instrumental harmony—
Love's voice is from all discord free,
Here darkly die, die darkly here,
And lack e'en Friendship's common tear;
A wreck of men, one score and ten,
And less thy hope than older men.

       [14] those [they 1905, 1907]

Autumn

Autumn grows old: he, like some simple one,
In Summer's castaway is strangely clad;
Such withered things the winds in frolic mad
Shake from his feeble hand and forehead wan.

Autumn is sighing for his early gold,
And in his tremble dropping his remains;
The brook talks more, as one bereft of brains,
Who singeth loud, delirious with the cold.

O now with drowsy June one hour to be!
Scarce waking strength to hear the hum of bees,
Or cattle lowing under shady trees,
Knee deep in waters loitering to the sea.

I would that drowsy June awhile were here,
The amorous South wind carrying all the vale—
Save that white lily true to star as pale,
Whose secret day-dream Phoebus burns to hear.[15]

Note: In the 1905 printing the second and third line of each stanza
were indented.

A Poet's Epitaph

Here lie the bones of Davies—William,
  Who always called the moon Phoebe,
And Phoebus always called the sun,
  And must, therefore, a poet be.

[15] hear [bear 1905]

8

'Twas one to him to sing in heaven,
    Or howl with demons in hell's pits,
To make himself at home, for he
    Was homeless here by starts and fits.

The world cursed him, and he cursed it,
    Till Death with dirt his throat did fill;
If e'er he wakes, he'll curse again,
    And worse—this Davies—William, will.

His granny oft foretold his fate,
    How he a ne'er-do-well would be;
'Twas well, maybe, she never heard
    The rascal call the moon Phoebe.

His grandad said—'He is a rogue.'
    'Not me, grandad,' said William's brother.
'Why, thou art fool!' their grandad roared.
    'Nay, young and simple both,' said mother.

The Cuckoo

Thou hide and seek, sly, jester bird,
    That lovest to startle solitude—
Wert thou not startled, cuckoo, too,
    To hear thy voice so close renewed?

Wert thou not waiting to make sure
    Nature in not a limb did move?
Or didst thou hope for that reply
    From Echo hiding in a grove?

I know not which most startled me,
    Thy voice which made me sudden stay,
Or Echo's voice which turned me round,
    To bring surprise another way.

No wonder thou art silent now,
    Since once thou madest thyself heard;
Thou knowest she will argue out,
    And, like her sex, will have last word.

Love Absent

Where wert thou, love, when from Twm Barlum turned
    The moon's face full thy way of Alterreen,
And from his wood's dark cage the nightingale
    Drave out clear notes across the open sheen?

I stood alone to see the ripples run
    From light to shade, and shade to light, in play;
Like fearsome children stealing guilty moves
    When Age is dozing—when thou wert away.

The banks of Alterreen are no less sweet,
    Nor Malpas Brook more chary of his flowers,
And I unchanged as they; but thou, dear love,
    Allowest Time to part us with his hours.

The Lodging House Fire

My birthday—yesterday,
Its hours were twenty-four;
Four hours I lived lukewarm,
And killed a score.

I woke eight times[16] and rose,
Came to our fire below,
Then sat four hours and watched
Its sullen glow.

    [16] times [chimes 1905, 1907]

Then out four hours I walked,
The lukewarm four I live,
And felt no other joy
Than air can give.

My mind durst know no thought
It knew my life too well:
'Twas hell before, behind,
And round me hell.

Back to that fire again,
Ten hours I watch it now,
And take to bed dim eyes,
And fever's brow.

Ten hours I give to sleep,
More than my need, I know;
But I escape my mind
And that fire's glow.

For listen: it is death
To watch that fire's glow;
For, as it burns more red
Men paler grow.

O better in foul room
That's warm, make life away,
Than homeless out of doors,
Cold night and day.

Pile on the coke, make fire,
Rouse its death-dealing glow;
Men are borne dead away
Ere they can know.

I lie; I cannot watch
Its glare from hour to hour;
It makes one sleep, to wake
Out of my power.

I close my eyes and swear
It shall not wield its power;
No use, I wake to find
A murdered hour

Lying between us there!
That fire drowsed me deep,
And I wrought murder's deed—
Did it in sleep.

I count us, thirty men,
Huddled from Winter's blow,
Helpless to move away
From that fire's glow.

So goes my life each day—
Its hours are twenty-four—
Four hours I live lukewarm,
And kill a score.

No man lives life so wise
But unto Time he throws
Morsels to hunger for
At his life's close.

Were all such morsels heaped—
Time greedily devours,
When man sits still—he'd mourn
So few wise hours.

But all my day is waste,
I live a lukewarm four
And make a red coke fire
Poison the score

Note: In its 1905 printing the second and fourth line of each
stanza were indented.

12

The Hill-side Park

Some banks cropped close, and lawns smooth mown and
    green,
Where, when a daisy's guiltless face was seen,
Its pretty head came sacrifice to pride
Of human taste—I saw upon the side
Of a steep hill. Without a branch of wood
Plants, giant-leaved, like boneless bodies stood.
The flowers had colonies, not one was seen
To go astray from its allotted green,
But to the light like mermaids' faces came
From waves of green, and scarce two greens the same.
And everywhere man's ingenuity
On fence and bordering: for I could see
The tiny scaffolding to hold the heads
And faces overgrown of flowers in beds
On which their weak-developed frames must fall,
Had they not such support upright and tall.
There was a fountain, and its waters' leap
Was under a full-quivered Cupid's keep.
And from his mother's lip[17] the spray was blown
Upon adjusted rock, selected stone;
And so was placed that all the waters fell
Into a small ravine in a small dell,
And made a stream, where that wee river raved,
As[18] gold his rocks and margent amber paved.
This park, it was a miracle of care,
But sweeter far to me the prospects there:
The far beyond, where lived Romance near seas
And pools in haze, and in far realms of trees.
I saw where Severn had run wide and free,
Out where the Holms lie flat upon a sea
Whose wrinkles wizard Distance smoothed away,
And still sails flecked its face of silver-grey.

The Ways of Time

As butterflies are but winged flowers,
    Half sorry for their change, who fain,
So still and long they lie on leaves,
    Would be thought flowers again—

E'en so my thoughts, that should expand,
    And grow to higher themes above,
Return like butterflies to lie
    On the old things I love.

The Likeness

When I came forth this morn I saw
    Quite twenty cloudlets in the air;
And then I saw a flock of sheep,
    Which told me how those clouds came there.

That flock of sheep, on that green grass,
    Well it might lie so still and proud!
Its likeness had been drawn in heaven,
    On a blue sky, in silvery cloud.

I gazed me up, I gazed me down,
    And swore, though good the likeness was,
'Twas a long way from justice done
    To such white wool, such sparkling grass.

The Distinction

This Talent is a slip, or shoot,
    Cut off the family tree;
To train with care and educate
    Which withers if let be.

But Genius is a seed that comes
    From where no man doth know;
Though left uncared, aye, hindered too,
    It cannot help but grow.

Talent's an outlet of Life's stream
    Whose waters know no change;
But Genius bringeth in from far
    New waters, sweet and strange.

Catharine

We children every morn would wait
For Catharine, at the garden gate;
Behind school-time, her sunny hair
Would melt the master's frown of care,
What time his hand but threatened pain,
Shaking aloft his awful cane;
So here one summer's morn we wait
For Catharine at the garden gate.
To Dave I say—'There's sure to be
Some coral isle unknown at sea,
And—if I see it first—'tis mine!
But I'll give it to Catharine.'
'When she grows up,' says Dave to me,
'Some ruler in a far countree,
Where every voice but his is dumb,
Owner of pearls, and gold, and gum,
Will build for her a shining throne,
Higher than his, and near his own;
And he, who would not list before,
Will listen to Catharine, and adore
Her face and form; and,' Dave went on—
When came a man there pale and wan,
Whose face was dark and wet though kind,

He, coming there, seemed like a wind
Whose breath is rain, yet will not stop
To give the parchèd flowers a drop:
'Go, children, to your school,' he said—
'And tell the master Catharine's dead.'

A Blind Child

Her baby brother laughed last night,
    The blind child asked her mother why;
    It was the light that caught his eye.
Would she might laugh to see that light!

The presence of a stiffened corse
    Is sad enough; but, to my mind,
    The presence of a child that's blind,
In a green garden, is far worse.

She felt my cloth—for worldly place;
    She felt my face—if I was good;
    My face lost more than half its blood,
For fear her hand would wrongly trace.

We're in the garden, where are bees
    And flowers, and birds, and butterflies;
    One greedy fledgling runs and cries
For all the food his parent sees!

I see them all: flowers of all kind,
    The sheep and cattle on the leas;
    The houses up the hills, the trees—
But I am dumb, for she is blind.

The Calm

A bird sings on yon apple bough,
And bees are humming near; and now
I think of my tempestuous past,
And wonder if these joys will last.
After a storm of many years,
There comes this calm to lay my fears.
In vain it comes: an anxious eye
Looks for a sign in every sky
For tempest; for it cannot be,
Methinks, that peace will stay with me.
Anon this mind forgets its past.
And then methinks this calm will last.
Then walk I down my lane to see
Sweet Primrose, pale Anemone.
Shy Violet, who hid from sight,
Until I followed a bee right
To her—now while the cries of Spring
Do make things grow, to run and leap.
But are these pleasant days to keep?
Where shall I be when Summer comes?
When with a bee's mouth closed, she hums
Sounds not to wake, but soft and deep,
To make her pretty charges sleep?
As long as Heaven is true to Earth,
Spring will not fail with her green growth,
Nor Autumn with his gold; but when
Troubles beset me, I seek men;
From Nature, with her flowers and songs,
To lose myself in human throngs;
From moonlit glade to limelit scene,
To playhouses from bowers green;
From mossy rock to painted mortar,
To Traffic's wheels from running water;
And from the birds' melodious calls
To lose myself in human brawls.

The Happiest Life

Take from the present hour its sweets;
For, as thou nearest Death's vast sea,
To empty thy Life's river there—
Thou wilt see flowerless banks of sand,
And naked rocks on that drear coast.

We rush through life as though it were
A race to grab new-opened land;
We live as though Life's pleasures were
Piled at its end, and when 'tis reached,
We moan them passed in years long gone.

We either do outrace old Time
Unto an end where no joys are,
Or lie us down in present ease,
In gluttony, or drunken sloth,
And make Time bear us sleeping on.

Man makes his life a burning fret,
Yet beasts do know a shady spot,
And know what herbs are good; proud man
Knows not how much, or what to eat,
And drinks fire-juice in Summer's prime.

We must clear out our vain desires,
Which covet more than gold can buy;
We must live more in Nature's way;
For what we want is th' drunkard's ease
Sans drugs to give us after pain.

We all are one at last; when Death
Hath glazed the eye of cruel Czar,
Which made so many mortals quail—
Bury it soon from flies. Ye gods,
Flies on that eye which cowed down men!

Facts

One night poor Jim had not a sou,
   Mike had enough for his own bed;
'Take it: I'll walk the streets to-night,'
   Said Mike, 'and you lie down instead.'

So Mike walked out, but ne'er came back;
   We know not whether he is drowned,
Or used his hands unlawfully;
   Is sick, or in some prison bound.

Now Jim was dying fast, and he
   Took to the workhouse his old bones;
To earn some water, bread, and sleep,
   They made that dying man break stones,

He swooned upon his heavy task:
   They carried him to a black coach,
And tearless strangers took him out—
   A corpse! at the infirmary's porch.

Since Jesus came with mercy and love,
   'Tis nineteen hundred years and five:
They made that dying man break stones,
   In faith that Christ is still alive.

New-comers

So many birds have come along,
The nightingale brings her sweet song,
With lease to charm, by her own self,
The nights of this best month in twelve.
To sit up all a night in June
With that sweet bird and a full moon—

The moon with all Heav'n for her worth,
The nightingale to have this earth,
And there we are for joy—we three.
And here's the swallow, wild and free,
Prince flyer of the air by day;
For doth he not, in human way,
Dive, float and use side strokes, like men
Swimming in some clear lake? And then,
See how he skates the iceless pond!
And lo! the lark springs from the land;
He sees a ladder to Heaven's gate,
And, step by step, without abate,
He mounts it singing, back and forth;
Till twenty steps or more from earth,
On his return, then without sound
He jumps, and stone-like drops to ground
And here are butterflies; poor things
Amazed with new-created wings;
They in the air-waves roll distrest
Like ships at sea; and when they rest
They cannot help but ope and close
Their wings, like babies with their toes.

The End of Summer

The Dandelion sails away,—
    Some other port for him next spring;
Since they have seen the harvest home,
    Sweet birds have little more to sing.

Since from her side the corn is ta'en,
    The Poppy thought to win some praise;
But birds sang ne'er a welcome note,
    So she blushed scarlet all her days.

The children strip the blackberry bush,
    And search the hedge for bitter sloe;
They bite the sloes, now sweet as plums—
    After Jack Frost had bit them so.

'Twas this Jack Frost, one week ago,
    Made watchdogs whine with fear and cold;
But all he did was make fruits smell,
    And make their coats to shine like gold.

No scattering force is in the wind,
    Though strong to shake the leaf from stem;
The leaves get in the rill's sweet throat,
    His voice is scarcely heard through them.

The darkest woods let in the light,
    And thin and frail are looking now;
And yet their weight is more than June's,
    Since nuts bend down each hazel bough.

Saturday Night in the Slums

Why do I stare at faces, why,
    Nor watch the happy children more?
Since Age has now a blackened eye,
    And that grey hair is stained with gore.

For an old woman passed, and she
    Would hide her face when I did stare,
But when she turns that face from me,
    There's clotted blood in her grey hair.

Aye, here was hell last night to play,
    The scream of children, murder cries;
When I came forth at early day,
    I saw old Age with blackened eyes.

Why do I stare at people so,
    Nor watch the little children more,
If one such brutal passions show,
    And joy is all the other's store?

O for the shot in some fierce land,
    A sword or dagger firmly held:
No brutal kick, no mauling hand,
    No horrors of the partly killed.

There is the man with brutal brow,
    The child with hunger's face of care:
The woman—it is something now
    If she lose pride to dress her hair.

I will give children my best hours,
    And of their simple ways will sing:
Just as a bird heeds less old flowers
    And sings his best to buds in spring.

Whiskey

Whiskey, thou blessèd heaven in the brain,
    O that the belly should revolt,
To make a hell of afterpain,
    And prove thy virtue was a fault!

Did ever poet seek his bed
    With a sweet phrase upon his lips
Smiling—as I laid down my head,
    Pleased after sundry whiskey sips?

I pitied all the world: alas
    That no poor nobodies came near,
To give to them my shirt and shoes,
    And bid them be of goodly cheer.

A blessèd heaven was in the brain;
  But ere came morn the belly turned
And kicked up hell's delight in pain—
  This tongue went dry, this throat it burned.

Oh dear! Oh dear! to think last night
  The merriest man on earth was I,
And that I should awake this morn,
  To cough and groan, to heave and sigh!

The Rain

I hear leaves drinking rain;
  I hear rich leaves on top
Giving the poor beneath
  Drop after drop;
'Tis a sweet noise to hear
These green leaves drinking near.

And when the Sun comes out,
  After this rain shall stop
A wondrous light will fill
  Each dark, round drop;
I hope the Sun shines bright;
'Twill be a lovely sight.

Robin Redbreast

Robin on a leafless bough,
  Lord in Heaven, how he sings!
Now cold Winter's cruel Wind
  Makes playmates of poor, dead things.

How he sings for joy this morn!
    How his breast doth pant and glow!
Look you how he stands and sings,
    Half-way up his legs in snow!

If these crumbs of bread were pearls,
    And I had no bread at home,
He should have them for that song;
    Pretty Robin Redbreast, Come.

The Wind

Sometimes he roars among the leafy trees
Such sounds as in a narrow cove, when Seas
Rush in between high rocks; or grandly roll'd,
Like music heard in churches that are old.
Sometimes he makes the children's happy sound,
When they play hide and seek, and one is found.
Sometimes he whineth like a dog in sleep,
Bit by the merciless, small fleas; then deep
And hollow sounds come from him, as starved men
Oft hear rise from their empty parts; and then
He'll hum a hollow groan, like one sick lain,
Who fears a move will but increase his pain.
And now he makes an awful wail, as when
From dark coal-pits are brought up crushed, dead men
To frantic wives. When he's on mischief bent,
He breeds more ill than that strange Parliament
Held by the witches, in the Hebrides;
He's here, he's there, to do whate'er he please.
For well he knows the spirits' tricks at night,
Of slamming doors, and blowing out our light,
And tapping at our windows, rattling pails,
And making sighs and moans, and shouts and wails.
'Twas he no doubt made that young man's hair white,

Who slept alone in a strange house one night,
And was an old man in the morn and crazed,
And all who saw and heard him were amazed.

Jenny

Now I grow old, and flowers are weeds,
    I think of days when weeds were flowers;
When Jenny lived across the way,
    And shared with me her childhood hours.

Her little teeth did seem so sharp,
    So bright and bold, when they were shown,
You'd think if passion stirred her she
    Could bite and hurt a man of stone.

Her curls, like golden snakes, would lie
    Upon each shoulder's front, as though
To guard her face on either side—
    They raised themselves when Winds did blow.

How sly they were! I could not see,
    Nor she feel them begin to climb
Across her lips, till there they were,
    To be forced back time after time.

If I could see an Elm in May
    Turn all his dark leaves into pearls,
And shake them in the light of noon—
    That sight had not shamed Jenny's curls.

And, like the hay, I swear her hair
    Was getting golder every day;
Yes, golder when 'twas harvested,
    Under a bonnet stacked away.

Ah, Jenny's gone, I know not where;
 Her face I cannot hope to see;
And every time I think of her
 The world seems one big grave to me.

Nature's Friend

Say what you like,
 All things love me!
I pick no flowers—
 That wins the Bee.

The Summer's Moths
 Think my hand one—
To touch their wings—
 With Wind and Sun.

The garden Mouse
 Comes near to play;
Indeed, he turns
 His eyes away.

The Wren knows well
 I rob no nest;
When I look in,
 She still will rest.

The hedge stops Cows,
 Or they would come
After my voice
 Right to my home.

The Horse can tell,
 Straight from my lip,
My hand could not
 Hold any whip.

Say what you like,
    All things love me!
Horse, Cow, and Mouse,
    Bird, Moth and Bee.

A Maiden and Her Hair

Her cruel hands go in and out,
    Like two pale woodmen working there,
To make a nut-brown thicket clear—
    The full, wild foliage of her hair.

Her hands now work far up the North
    Then, fearing for the South's extreme,
They into her dark waves of hair
    Dive down so quick—it seems a dream.

They're in the light again with speed,
    Tossing the loose hair to and fro,
Until, like tamèd snakes, the coils
    Lie on her bosom in a row.

For wise inspection, up and down
    One coil her busy hands now run;
To screw and twist, to turn and shape,
    And here and there to work like one.

And now those white hands, still like one,
    Are working at the perilous end;
Where they must knot those nut-brown coils,
    Which will hold fast, though still they'll bend.

Sometimes one hand must fetch strange tools,
    The other then must work alone;
But when more instruments are brought,
    See both make up the time that's gone.

Now that her hair is bound secure,
Coil top of coil, in smaller space,
Ah, now I see how smooth her brow,
And her simplicity of face.

Early Morn

When I did wake this morn from sleep,
It seemed I heard birds in a dream;
Then I arose to take the air—
The lovely air that made birds scream;
Just as green hill launched the ship
Of gold, to take its first clear dip.

And it began its journey then,
As I came forth to take the air;
The timid Stars had vanished quite,
The Moon was dying with a stare;
Horses, and kine, and sheep were seen
As still as pictures, in fields green.

It seemed as though I had surprised
And trespassed in a golden world
That should have passed while men still slept!
The joyful birds, the ship of gold,
The horses, kine and sheep did seem
As they would vanish for a dream.

A Beggar's Life

When farmers sweat and toil at ploughs,
The wives give me cool milk and sweet;
When merchants in their office brood,
Their ladies give me cakes to eat,

And hot tea for my happy blood;
  This is a jolly life indeed,
  To do no work and get my need.

I have no child for future thought,
  I feed no belly but my own,
And I can sleep when toilers fail;
  Content, though sober, sleeps on stone,
But Care can't sleep with down and ale;
  This is a happy life indeed,
  To do no work and get my need.

I trouble not for pauper's grave,
  There is no feeling after death;
The king will be as deaf to praise
  As I to blame—when this world saith
A word of us in after days;
  It is a jolly life indeed,
  To do no work and get my need.

School's Out

  Girls scream,
    Boys shout;
  Dogs bark,
    School's out.

  Cats run,
    Horses shy;
  Into trees
    Birds fly.

  Babes wake
    Open-eyed;
  If they can,
    Tramps hide.

Old man,
    Hobble home;
Merry mites,
    Welcome.

A Happy Life

O what a life is this I lead,
Far from the hum of human greed;
Where Crows, like merchants dressed in black,
Go leisurely to work and back;
Where Swallows leap and dive and float,
And Cuckoo sounds his cheerful note;
Where Skylarks now in clouds do rave,
Half mad with fret that their souls have
By hundreds far more joyous notes
Than they can manage with their throats.

The ploughman's heavy horses run
The field as if in fright—for fun,
Or stand and laugh in voices shrill;
Or roll upon their backs until
The sky's kicked small enough—they think;
Then to a pool they go and drink.
The kine are chewing their old cud,
Dreaming, and never think to add
Fresh matter that will taste—as they
Lie motionless, and dream away.

I hear the sheep a-coughing near;
Like little children, when they hear
Their elders' sympathy—so these
Sheep force their coughs on me, and please;
And many a pretty lamb I see,
Who stops his play on seeing me,

And runs and tells his mother then.
Lord, who would live in towns with men.
And hear the hum of human greed—
With such a life as this to lead?

City and Country

The City has dull eyes,
  The City's cheeks are pale;
The City has black spit,
  The City's breath is stale.

The Country has red cheeks,
  The Country's eyes are bright;
The Country has sweet breath,
  The Country's spit is white.

Dull eyes, breath stale; ink spit
  And cheeks like chalk—for thee;
Eyes bright, red cheeks; sweet breath
  And spit like milk—for me.

A Merry Hour

As long as I see Nature near,
I will, when old, cling to life dear:
E'en as the old dog holds so fast
With his three teeth, which are his last.
For Lord, how merry now am I!
Tickling with straw the Butterfly,
Where she doth in her clean, white dress,
Sit on a green leaf, motionless,
To hear Bees hum away the hours.

I shake those Bees too off the Flowers,
So that I may laugh soft to hear
Their hoarse resent and angry stir.
I hear the sentry Chanticleer
Challenge each other far and near,
From farm to farm, and it rejoices
Me this hour to mock their voices;
There's one red Sultan near me now,
Not all his wives make half his row.
Cuckoo! Cuckoo! was that a bird,
Or but a mocking boy you heard?
You heard the Cuckoo first, 'twas he;
The second time—Ha, ha! 'twas Me.

Truly Great

My walls outside must have some flowers,
　My walls within must have some books;
A house that's small; a garden large,
　And in it leafy nooks.

A little gold that's sure each week;
　That comes not from my living kind,
But from a dead man in his grave,
　Who cannot change his mind.

A lovely wife, and gentle too;
　Contented that no eyes but mine
Can see her many charms, nor voice
　To call her beauty fine.

Where she would in that stone cage live,
　A self-made prisoner, with me;
While many a wild bird sang around,
　On gate, on bush, on tree.

And she sometimes to answer them,
    In her far sweeter voice than all;
Till birds, that loved to look on leaves,
    Will doat on a stone wall.

With this small house, this garden large,
    This little gold, this lovely mate,
With health in body, peace at heart—
    Show me a man more great.

The Laughers

Mary and Maud have met at the door,
    Oh, now for a din; I told you so:
They're laughing at once with sweet, round mouths,
    Laughing for what? does anyone know?

Is it known to the bird in the cage,
    That shrieketh for joy his high top notes,
After a silence so long and grave—
    What started at once those two sweet throats?

Is it known to the Wind that he takes
    Advantage at once and comes right in?
Is it known to the cock in the yard,
    That crows—the cause of that merry din?

Is it known to the babe that he shouts?
    Is it known to the old, purring cat?
Is it known to the dog, that he barks
    For joy—what Mary and Maud laugh at?

Is it known to themselves? It is not,
    But beware of their great shining eyes;
For Mary and Maud will soon, I swear,
    Find a cause to make far merrier cries.

Australian Bill

Australian Bill is dying fast,
　　For he's a drunken fool:
He either sits in an alehouse,
　　Or stands outside a school.

He left this house of ours at seven,
　　And he was drunk by nine;
And when I passed him near a school
　　He nods his head to mine.

When Bill took to the hospital,
　　Sick, money he had none—
He came forth well, but lo! his home,
　　His wife and child had gone.

'I'll watch a strange school every day,
　　Until the child I see;
For Liz will send the child to school—
　　No doubt of that,' says he.

And 'Balmy' Tom is near as bad,
　　A-drinking ale till blind:
No absent child grieves he, but there's
　　A dead love on his mind.

But Bill, poor Bill, is dying fast,
　　For he's the greater fool;
He either sits in an alehouse
　　Or stands outside a school.

A Lovely Woman

Now I can see what Helen was:
Men cannot see this woman pass
And be not stirred; as Summer's Breeze

Sets leaves in battle on the trees.
A woman moving gracefully,
With golden hair enough for three,
Which, mercifully! is not loose,
But lies in coils to her head close;
With lovely eyes, so dark and blue,
So deep, so warm, they burn me through.
I see men follow her, as though
Their homes were where her steps should go.
She seemed as sent to our cold race
For fear the beauty of her face
Made Paradise in flames like Troy—
I could have gazed all day with joy.
In fancy I could see her stand
Before a savage, fighting band,
And make them, with her words and looks,
Exchange their spears for shepherds' crooks,
And sing to sheep in quiet nooks;
In fancy saw her beauty make
A thousand gentle priests uptake
Arms for her sake, and shed men's blood.
The fairest piece of womanhood,
Lovely in feature, form and grace,
I ever saw, in any place.

Money

When I had money, money, O!
   I knew no joy till I went poor;
For many a false man as a friend
   Came knocking all day at my door.

Then felt I like a child that holds
   A trumpet that he must not blow
Because a man is dead; I dared
   Not speak to let this false world know.

Much have I thought of life, and seen
  How poor men's hearts are ever light;
And how their wives do hum like bees
  About their work from morn till night.

So, when I hear these poor ones laugh,
  And see the rich ones coldly frown—
Poor men, think I, need not go up
  So much as rich men should come down.

When I had money, money, O!
  My many friends proved all untrue;
But now I have no money, O!
  My friends are real, though very few.

Where we Differ

To think my thoughts all hers,
  Not one of hers is mine;
She laughs—while I must sigh;
  She sings—while I must whine.

She eats—while I must fast;
  She reads—while I am blind;
She sleeps—while I must wake;
  Free—I no freedom find.

To think the world for me
  Contains but her alone,
And that her eyes prefer
  Some ribbon, scarf, or stone.

The Sea

Her cheeks were white, her eyes were wild,
Her heart was with her sea-gone child.
'Men say you know and love the sea?
It is ten days, my child left me;
Ten days, and still he doth not come,
And I am weary of my home.'

I thought of waves that ran the deep
And flashed like rabbits, when they leap,
The white part of their tails; the glee
Of captains that take brides to sea,
And own the ships they steer; how seas
Played leapfrog over ships with ease.

The great Sea-Wind, so rough and kind;
Ho, ho! his strength; the great Sea-Wind
Blows iron tons across the sea!
Ho, ho! his strength; how wild and free!
He breaks the waves, to our amaze,
Into ten thousand little sprays!

'Nay, have no fear'; I laughed with joy,
'That you have lost a sea-gone boy;
The Sea's wild horses, they are far
More safe than Land's tamed horses are;
They kick with padded hoofs, and bite
With teeth that leave no marks in sight.

'True, Waves will howl when, all day long,
The Wind keeps piping loud and strong;
For in ships' sails the wild Sea-Breeze
Pipes sweeter than your birds in trees;
But have no fear'—I laughed with joy,
'That you have lost a sea-gone boy.'

That night I saw ten thousand bones
Coffined in ships, in weeds and stones;
Saw how the Sea's strong jaws could take
Big iron ships like rats to shake;
Heard him still moan his discontent
For one man or a continent.

I saw that woman go from place
To place, hungry for her child's face;
I heard her crying, crying, crying;
Then, in a flash! saw the Sea trying,
With savage joy, and efforts wild,
To smash his rocks with a dead child.

The Dark Hour

And now, when merry winds do blow,
    And rain makes trees look fresh,
An overpowering staleness holds
    This mortal flesh.

Though I do love to feel the rain,
    And be by winds well blown—
The mystery of mortal life
    Doth press me down.

And, in this mood, come now what will,
    Shine Rainbow, Cuckoo call;
There is no thing in Heaven or Earth
    Can lift my soul.

I know not where this state comes from—
    No cause for grief I know;
The Earth around is fresh and green,
    Flowers near me grow.

I sit between two fair Rose trees;
    Red roses on my right,
And on my left side roses are
    A lovely white.

The little birds are full of joy,
    Lambs bleating all the day;
The colt runs after the old mare,
    And children play.

And still there comes this dark, dark hour—
    Which is not born of Care;
Into my heart it creeps before
    I am aware.

Jenny Wren

Her sight is short, she comes quite near;
A foot to me's a mile to her;
And she is known as Jenny Wren,
The smallest bird in England. When
I heard that little bird at first,
Methought her frame would surely burst
With earnest song. Oft had I seen
Her running under leaves so green,
Or in the grass when fresh and wet,
As though her wings she would forget.
And, seeing this, I said to her—
'My pretty runner, you prefer
To be a thing to run unheard
Through leaves and grass, and not a bird!'
'Twas then she burst, to prove me wrong,
Into a sudden storm of song;
So very loud and earnest, I
Feared she would break her heart and die.

'Nay, nay,' I laughed, 'be you no thing
To run unheard, sweet scold, but sing!
O I could hear your voice near me,
Above the din in that oak tree,
When almost all the twigs on top
Had starlings singing without stop.'

The Idiot and the Child

There was a house where an old dame
    Lived with a son, his child and wife;
And with a son of fifty years,
    An idiot all his life.

When others wept this idiot laughed,
    When others laughed he then would weep:
The married pair took oath his eyes
    Did never close in sleep.

Death came that way, and which, think you,
    Fell under that old tyrant's spell?
He breathed upon that little child,
    Who loved her life so well.

This made the idiot chuckle hard:
    The old dame looked at that child dead
And him she loved—'Ah, well; thank God
    It is no worse!' she said.

Now

When I was in yon town, and had
    Stones all round me, hard and cold,
My flesh was firm, my sight was keen,
    And still I felt my heart grow old.

But now, with this green world around,
   By my great love for it! I swear,
Though my flesh shrink, and my sight fail,
   My heart will not grow old with care.

When I do hear these joyful birds,
   I cannot sit with my heart dumb;
I cannot walk among these flowers,
   But I must help the bees to hum.

My heart has echoes for all things,
   The wind, the rain, the bird and bee;
'Tis I that—now—can carry Time,
   Who in that town must carry me.

I see not now the great coke fire
   With ten men seated there, or more,
Like frogs on logs; and one man fall
   Dying across the boarded floor.

I see instead the flowers and clouds,
   I hear the rills, the birds and bees:
The Squirrel flies before the storm
   He makes himself in leafy trees.

Rose

Sweet Margaret's laugh can make
Her whole plump body shake.

Jane's cherry lips can show
Their white stones in a row.

A soft June smile steals out
Of Mary's April pout.

Sweet creatures swim and play
In Maud's blue pools all day.

But when Rose walks abroad,
Jane, Margaret, Mary, Maud,

Do stand as little chance
To throw a lovely glance,

As the Moon that's in the sky
While still the Sun is high.

The Green Tent

Summer has spread a cool, green tent
    Upon the bare poles of this tree;
Where 'tis a joy to sit all day,
    And hear the small birds' melody;
To see the sheep stand bolt upright,
    Nibbling at grass almost their height.

And much I marvel now how men
    Can waste their fleeting days in greed;
That one man should desire more gold
    Than twenty men should truly need;
For is not this green tent more sweet
    Than any chamber of the great?

This tent, at which I spend my day,
    Was made at Nature's cost, not mine;
And when night comes, and I must sleep,
    No matter if my room be fine
Or common, for Content and Health
    Can sleep without the power of Wealth.

Selfish Hearts

Without a thought
   If death brings in
Joy for our virtue,
   Pain for our sin—

Know this hard truth:
   They live on earth
The sweetest life,
   Who, rich from birth,

Do then maintain
   A selfish mind;
To moans are deaf,
   To tears are blind.

Weep for the poor
   You find in books:
From living poor
   Avert your looks.

Then dance and sing,
   Dress, sail or ride;
Go in your coach
   To halls of Pride.

A selfish heart,
   And rich from birth,
No sweeter life
   Can be on earth.

To match the joy,
   There lives but one:
The beggar who
   Lives all alone.

With selfish heart,
    And shameless, he
Begs bread at huts,
    And almshouse tea.

O selfish pair!
    I know not which
Is happiest—
    So poor, or rich.

The decent poor,
    The working mass,
In misery
    Their lives must pass.

No Master

Indeed this is sweet life! my hand
Is under no proud man's command;
There is no voice to break my rest
Before a bird has left its nest;
There is no man to change my mood,
Would I go nutting in the wood;
No man to pluck my sleeve and say—
I want thy labour for this day;
No man to keep me out of sight,
When that dear Sun is shining bright.
None but my friends shall have command
Upon my time, my heart and hand;
I'll rise from sleep to help a friend,
But let no stranger orders send,
Or hear my curses fast and thick,
Which in his purse-proud throat will stick
Like burrs. If I cannot be free
To do such work as pleases me,

Near woodland pools and under trees,
You'll get no work at all; for I
Would rather live this life and die
A beggar or a thief, than be
A working slave with no days free.

On the Death of a little Child

Her pretty dances were her own,
    Her songs were by no other sung;
And all the laughter in her house
    Was started by her own sweet tongue.

This little dance and song composer,
    This laughter maker, sweet and small,
Will never more be seen or heard—
    For her the Sexton's bell does toll.

The shining eyes are closed for aye,
    And that small, crimson mouth of mirth;
The little feet, the little hands—
    All stiff and cold inside the earth.

Clouds

My Fancy loves to play with Clouds
    That hour by hour can change Heaven's face;
For I am sure of my delight,
    In green or stony place.

Sometimes they on tall mountains pile
    Mountains of silver, twice as high;
And then they break and lie like rocks
    All over the wide sky.

And then I see flocks very fair;
   And sometimes, near their fleeces white,
Are small, black lambs that soon will grow
   And hide their mothers quite.

Sometimes, like little fishes, they
   Are all one size, and one great shoal;
Sometimes they, like big sailing ships,
   Across the blue sky roll.

Sometimes I see small Cloudlets tow
   Big, heavy Clouds across those skies—
Like little Ants that carry off
   Dead Moths ten times their size.

Sometimes I see at morn bright Clouds
   That stand so still, they make me stare;
It seems as they had trained all night
   To make no motion there.

In the Country

This life is sweetest; in this wood
I hear no children cry for food;
I see no woman, white with care;
No man, with muscles wasting here.

No doubt it is a selfish thing
To fly from human suffering;
No doubt he is a selfish man,
Who shuns poor creatures sad and wan.

But 'tis a wretched life to face
Hunger in almost every place;
Cursed with a hand that's empty, when
The heart is full to help all men.

Can I admire the statue great,
When living men starve at its feet?
Can I admire the park's green tree,
A roof for homeless misery?

When I can see few men in need,
I then have power to help by deed,
Nor lose my cheerfulness in pity—
Which I must do in every city.

For when I am in those great places,
I see ten thousand suffering faces;
Before me stares a wolfish eye,
Behind me creeps a groan or sigh.

The Kingfisher

It was the Rainbow gave thee birth,
    And left thee all her lovely hues;
And, as her mother's name was Tears,
    So runs it in my[19] blood to choose
For haunts the lonely pools, and keep
In company with trees that weep.

Go you and, with such glorious hues,
    Live with proud Peacocks in green parks;
On lawns as smooth as shining glass,
    Let every feather show its marks;
Get thee on boughs and clap thy wings
Before the windows of proud kings.

Nay, lovely Bird, thou art not vain;
    Thou hast no proud, ambitious mind;
I also love a quiet place
    That's green, away from all mankind;
A lonely pool, and let a tree
Sigh with her bosom over me.

[19] my [thy 1910]

47

The Sluggard

A jar of cider and my pipe,
　　In summer, under shady tree;
A book of one that made his mind
　　Live by its sweet simplicity:
Then must I laugh at kings who sit
　　In richest chambers, signing scrolls;
And princes cheered in public ways,
　　And stared at by a thousand fools.

Let me be free to wear my dreams,
　　Like weeds in some mad maiden's hair,
When she doth think the earth has not
　　Another maid so rich and fair;
And proudly smiles on rich and poor,
　　The queen of all fair women then:
So I, dressed in my idle dreams,
　　Will think myself the king of men.

Old Ragan

Who lives in this black wooden hut?
　　Old Ragan lives there, all alone;
He cursed a lovely lady once,
　　Who let her shadow cross his own.

His tongue is a perpetual spring
　　Of oaths that never cease to drop;
Wouldst hear him swear? Speak kindly thus,
　　'Good morning, Ragan'—and then stop.

Sometimes a woman thoughtlessly
　　Has greeted Ragan in this way;
And she will not forget his look
　　And language till her dying day.

He throws his fowls their own eggshells,
　　Feeds them on thrice-boiled leaves of tea;
And dead flies on his window-sill,
　　He killed when they danced merrily.

A wicked, mean, suspicious man,
　　He growls to hear an infant's noise;
He hides behind the walls and trees,
　　To frighten little girls and boys.

What made old Ragan come to this?
　　Young men did jeer at him and shout;
So women, children and houseflies
　　Must bear the old man's vengeance out.

The Call of the Sea

Gone are the days of canvas sails!
No more great sailors tell their tales
In country taverns, barter pearls
For kisses from strange little girls;
And when the landlord's merry daughter
Heard their rough jokes and shrieked with laughter,
They threw a muffler of rare fur,
That hid her neck from ear to ear.
Ho, ho! my merry men; they know
Where gold is plentiful—Sail ho!
How they did love the rude wild Sea!
The rude, unflattering Sea; for he
Will not lie down for monarch's yacht,
No more than merchant's barge; he'll not
Keep graves with marks of wood or stone
For fish or fowl, or human bone.
The Sea is loth to lose a friend;
Men of one voyage, who did spend

Six months with him, hear his vexed cry
Haunting their houses till they die.
And for the sake of him they let
The winds blow them, and raindrops wet
Their foreheads with fresh water sprays—
Thinking of his wild, salty days.
And well they love to saunter near
A river, and its motion hear;
And see ships lying in calm beds,
That danced upon seas' living heads;
And in their dreams they hear again
Men's voices in a hurricane—
Like ghosts complaining that their graves
Are moved by sacrilegious waves.
And they do love to stand and hear
The old seafaring men that fear
Land more than water; carts and trains
More than wild waves and hurricanes.
And they do walk with love and pride
The tattooed mariner beside—
Chains, anchors on his arm, and Ships[20]—
And listen to his bearded lips.
Aye, they will hear the Sea's vexed cry
Haunting their houses till they die.

The Example

Here's an example from
    A Butterfly;
That on a rough, hard rock
    Happy can lie;
Friendless and all alone
On this unsweetened stone.

[20] Ships [ships 1910, 1928]

Now let my bed be hard,
　No care take I;
I'll make my joy like this
　Small Butterfly;
Whose happy heart has power
To make a stone a flower.

Leisure

What is this life if, full of care,
We have no time to stand and stare.

No time to stand beneath the boughs
And stare as long as sheep or cows.

No time to see, when woods we pass,
Where squirrels hide their nuts in grass.

No time to see, in broad daylight,
Streams full of stars like[21] skies at night.

No time to turn at Beauty's glance,
And watch her feet, how they can dance.

No time to wait till her mouth can
Enrich that smile her eyes began.

A poor life this if, full of care,
We have no time to stand and stare.

[21] stars like [stars, like 1911, 1928]

Fancy's Home

Tell me, Fancy, sweetest child,
    Of thy parents and thy birth;
Had they silk, and had they gold
    And a park to wander forth,
With a castle green and old?

In a cottage I was born,
    My kind father was Content,
My dear mother Innocence;
    On wild fruits of wonderment
I have nourished ever since.

Sheep

When I was once in Baltimore,
    A man came up to me and cried,
'Come, I have eighteen hundred sheep,
    And we will sail on Tuesday's tide.

'If you will sail with me, young man,
    I'll pay you fifty shillings down;
These eighteen hundred sheep I take
    From Baltimore to Glasgow town.'

He paid me fifty shillings down,
    I sailed with eighteen hundred sheep;
We soon had cleared the harbour's mouth,
    We soon were in the salt sea deep.

The first night we were out at sea
    Those sheep were quiet in their mind;
The second night they cried with fear—
    They smelt no pastures in the wind.

They sniffed, poor things, for their green fields,
　　They cried so loud I could not sleep:
For fifty thousand shillings down
　　I would not sail again with sheep.

Days that have Been

Can I forget the sweet days that have been,
　　When poetry first began to warm my blood;
When from the hills of Gwent I saw the earth
　　Burned into two by Severn's silver flood:

When I would go alone at night to see
　　The moonlight, like a big white butterfly,
Dreaming on that old castle near Caerleon,
　　While at its side the Usk went softly by:

When I would stare at lovely clouds in Heaven,
　　Or watch them when reported by deep streams;
When feeling pressed like thunder, but would not
　　Break into that grand music of my dreams?

Can I forget the sweet days that have been,
　　The villages so green I have been in;
Llantarnam, Magor, Malpas, and Llanwern,
　　Liswery, old Caerleon, and Alteryn?

Can I forget the banks of Malpas Brook,
　　Or Ebbw's voice in such a wild delight,
As on he dashed with pebbles in his throat,
　　Gurgling towards the sea with all his might?

Ah, when I see a leafy village now,
　　I sigh and ask it for Llantarnam's green;
I ask each river where is Ebbw's voice—
　　In memory of the sweet days that have been.

To a Working Man

You working man, of what avail
    Are these fine teachings of the great,
    To raise you to a better state;
When you forget in pots of ale
    That slavery's not your common fate.

You victim to all fraud and greed,
    Shun now that mind-destroying state:
    Go, meet your masters in debate:
Go home from work and think and read—
    To make our laws is your true fate.

Treasures

He hailed me with a cheerful voice,
    I answered him with ready lips;
As though we sailed the briny seas,
    And hailed from passing ships.

'Come in,' quoth he, 'and I will show
    Thee treasures few men saw before.'
He from his pocket took a key
    And opened wide his door.

He seemed no more than other men,
    His voice was calm, his eyes were cold;
He was not tall, he was not short,
    Nor seemed he young nor old.

I'll see some treasures now, methought—
    Some work in silk and ivory;
Some painted trays and vases quaint,
    Things with a history.

I saw at once some glittering beads
    That seemed like berries fit to eat;
Such as make children leave the woods
    Crying for their home sweet.

'Aye, aye,' quoth he, 'a little maid
    Played with them fifty years ago;
She's perished on the scaffold since—
    That's why I prize them so.

'Pray sit thee down in comfort now,
    For I have treasures rich and rare.'
He went upstairs, I sat me down
    And round the room did stare.

That room looked strange; a little fire,
    The lamp burned low, the hour was late;
A horse outside cropped grass—the sound
    Seemed like the steps of Fate.

The furniture in that man's room
    Seemed part of one large, deadly plant
Which if I touched would hold me fast,
    To perish soon of want.

Aye, I confess, I trembling stayed,
    Thralled by an unexplained desire;
I shook like negro in his hut,
    Sick at a little fire.

I heard him tumbling things about,
    Methought I heard a murder call
And blows; and then the blows did cease—
    I heard a body fall.

Then all was still, how still it was!
    I heard him breathing hard; at last
I heard him with a load caught in
    The narrow stairway fast.

And now he shows his face again;
   I see a bundle on his arm,
A dress, a sheet, a boot—and things
   Too simple to alarm.

'Now list,' quoth he, 'I told thee once
   That I had treasures rich and rare:
This sheet did smother a small babe,
   It was a baron's heir.

'This long, black dress a poisoner wore—
   Her head was chopped off with an axe;
'Tis priceless unto those that made
   Her figure show in wax.

'This is the boot, one of a pair,
   The other matters not'—he said;
''Twas with this boot a murderer kicked
   To bits his dead man's head.

'These bones were found upon a raft,
   And brought to shore by seamen true:
Bones of a little boy, picked clean
   By a cannibal crew.

'When Bill Black murdered Liza Green,
   As she sat down to pickled pork,
He finished her sweet supper with
   This very knife and fork.

'This scarf, which ties them all in one,
   Was my own father's, he one day
Hanged himself to a beam by it—
   I've other things, so prithee stay.'

He whistling went upstairs again,
   I softly crept towards the door
And vanished in the night, nor saw,
   Nor wished to see him more.

Beauty's Revenge

Proud Margery rang her peal of bells;
  'If you despise all womankind,
Take care, young man,' she said, 'take care
  No woman ever plagues your mind'—
The young man smoothed his own soft hair.

And how it came about, who knows,
  It is for womankind to tell;
Before a full-blown rose could fade,
  That man was suffering passion's hell
For Margery, that merry maid.

She brought ripe cherries to his sleep,
  Her teeth and eyes they shone at night;
'I am,' he murmured in his dreams,
  'A poor black ruin blessed with light—
From Margery come those heavenly beams.'

He dreamt he saw her hair at hand;
  'My soul,' he sighed, 'is little worth,
My life till now had little hope,
  But I will find my heaven on earth
By holding to this silken rope.'

He told his love to Margery soon,
  She bird-like cocked her cruel head,
She rang her peal of bells again:
  'Nay, I despise you men,' she said—
'Good-bye, young man, and take no pain.'

Days too Short

When primroses are out in Spring,
   And small, blue violets come between;
   When merry birds sing on boughs green,
And rills, as soon as born, must sing;

When butterflies will make side-leaps,
   As though escaped from Nature's hand
   Ere perfect quite; and bees will stand
Upon their heads in fragrant deeps;

When small clouds are so silvery white
   Each seems a broken rimmèd moon—
   When such things are, this world too soon,
For me, doth wear the veil of Night.

The Temper of a Maid

The Swallow dives in yonder air,
The Robin sings with sweetest ease,
The Apple shines among the leaves,
The Leaf is dancing in the breeze;
The Butterfly's on a warm stone,
The Bee is suckled by a flower;
The Wasp's inside a ripe red plum,
The Ant has found his load this hour;
The Squirrel counts and hides his nuts,
The Stoat is on a scent that burns;
The Mouse is nibbling a young shoot,
The Rabbit sits beside his ferns;
The Snake has found a sunny spot,
The Frog and Snail a slimy shade;
But I can find no joy on earth,
All through the temper of a maid.

Christ, the Man

Lord, I say nothing; I profess
   No faith in thee nor Christ thy Son:
Yet no man ever heard me mock
   A true believing one.

If knowledge is not great enough
   To give a man believing power,
Lord, he must wait in thy great hand
   Till revelation's hour.

Meanwhile he'll follow Christ, the man
   In that humanity he taught,
Which to the poor and the oppressed
   Gives its best time and thought.

The Grey-haired Child

Thy father was a drunken man,
   He threatened thee with a sharp knife;
And thou, a child not ten years old,
   Lay trembling for thy life.

Lay trembling in the dark all night,
   Sleep could not seal thine eye or ear;
Thy hair, which was a dark rich brown,
   Is now made grey by fear.

A Mother's Science

I heard a man once say this world
   Was but a speck in space;
A leaf upon a shoreless tide,
   That had no resting-place.

I told him then how vast this world
   Was to my own poor mind;
Of all the places seen, and still
   My child I could not find.

I told that man where I had been,
   I mentioned towns around;
And still my boy, in all these years,
   Is never to be found.

The East in Gold

Somehow this world is wonderful at times,
   As it has been from early morn in May;
Since first I heard the cock-a-doodle-do—
   Timekeeper on green farms—at break of day.

Soon after that I heard ten thousand birds,
   Which made me think an angel brought a bin
Of golden grain, and none was scattered yet—
   To rouse those birds to make that merry din.

I could not sleep again, for such wild cries,
   And went out early into their green world;
And then I saw what set their little tongues
   To scream for joy—they saw the East in gold.

Circumstance

Down in the deep salt sea
   A mighty fish will make
Its own strong current, which
   The little ones must take;
Which they must follow still,
No matter for their will.

Here, in this human sea,
    Is Circumstance, that takes
Men where they're loth to go;
    It fits them false and makes
Machines of master souls,
And masters of dull fools.

Slum Children

Your songs at night a drunkard sings,
    Stones, sticks and rags your daily flowers;
Like fishes' lips, a bluey white,
    Such lips, poor mites, are yours.

Poor little things, so sad and solemn,
    Whose lives are passed in human crowds—
When in the water I can see
    Heaven with a flock of clouds.

Poor little mites that breathe foul air,
    Where garbage chokes the sink and drain—
Now when the hawthorn smells so sweet,
    Wet with the summer rain.

But few of ye will live for long;
    Ye are but small new islands seen,
To disappear before your lives
    Can grow and be made green.

To Sparrows Fighting

Stop, feathered bullies!
  Peace, angry birds;
You common Sparrows that,
  For a few words,
Roll fighting in wet mud,
To shed each other's blood.

Look at those Linnets, they
  Like ladies sing;
See how those Swallows, too,
  Play on the wing;
All other birds close by
Are gentle, clean and shy.

And yet maybe your life's
  As sweet as theirs;
The common poor that fight
  Live not for years
In one long frozen state
Of anger, like the great.

The Two Flocks

Where are you going to now, white sheep,
  Walking the green hill-side;
To join that whiter flock on top,
  And share their pride?

Stay where you are, you silly sheep:
  When you arrive up there,
You'll find that whiter flock on top
  Clouds in the air!

A Dream

I met her in the leafy woods,
    Early a Summer's night;
I saw her white teeth in the dark,
    There was no better light.

Had she not come up close and made
    Those lilies their light spread,
I had not proved her mouth a rose,
    So round, so fresh, so red.

Her voice was gentle, soft and sweet,
    In words she was not strong;
Yet her low twitter had more charm
    Than any full-mouthed song.

We walked in silence to her cave,
    With but few words to say;
But ever and anon she stopped
    For kisses on the way.

And after every burning kiss
    She laughed and danced around;
Back-bending, with her breasts straight up,
    Her hair it touched the ground.

When we lay down, she held me fast,
    She held me like a leech;
Ho, ho! I know what her red tongue
    Is made for, if not speech.[22]

[22] Following stanza omitted. [Into my mouth it goes with mine,/I felt its soft warm waves;/That fair Enchantress knew full well/The way to make men slaves. 1911]

And what is this, how strange, how sweet!
   Her teeth are made to bite
The man she gives her passion to,
   And not to boast their white.

O night of Joy! O morning's grief!
   For when, with passion done,
Rocked on her breast I fell asleep,
   I woke, and lay alone.

The Heap of Rags

One night when I went down
Thames' side, in London Town,
A heap of rags saw I,
And sat me down close by.
That thing could shout and bawl,
But showed no face at all;
When any steamer passed
And blew a loud shrill blast,
That heap of rags would sit
And make a sound like it;
When struck the clock's deep bell,
It made those peals as well.
When winds did moan around,
It mocked them with that sound.
When all was quiet, it
Fell into a strange fit;
Would sigh, and moan and roar,
It laughed, and blessed, and swore.
Yet that poor thing, I know,
Had neither friend nor foe;
Its blessing or its curse
Made no one better or worse.
I left it in that place—
The thing that showed no face,

Was it a man that had
Suffered till he went mad?
So many showers and not
One rainbow in the lot;
Too many bitter fears
To make a pearl from tears.

Fairies, Take Care

A thousand blessings, Puck, on you
For knotting that long grass which threw
Into my arms a maid; for we
Have told our love and kissed, and she
Will lie a-bed in a sweet fright.
So, all ye Fairies who to-night
May take that stormy passage where
Her bosom's quicksands are, take care
Of whirlpools too: beware all you
Of that great tempest Love must brew.
The waves will rock your breath near out;
First sunk, then tossed and rolled about,
Now on your heads, now on your feet—
You'll be near swamped and, for life sweet,
Be glad to cross that stormy main,
And stand on something firm again.
Would I could see her while she sleeps,
And smiles to feel you climb those steeps,
Where you at last will stand up clear
Upon their cherry tops, and cheer.
And that ye are not lost, take care,
In that deep forest of her hair:
Yet ye may enter naked stark,
It gets more warm as it gets dark.
So, Fairies, fear not any harm,
While in those woods so dark and warm.

Captives

In this deep hollow, lying down,
    I, looking up at Heaven, can see
You pretty little clouds shut in
    By green hills all around—like me.

And all you simple, little clouds
    Seem glad at my captivity:
Without a thought that I can smile
    As much at you as you at me.

The Little Ones

The little ones are put in bed,
    And both are laughing, lying down;
Their father, and their mother too,
    Are gone on Christmas eve to town.

'Old Santa Claus will bring a horse,
    Gee up:' cried little Will, with glee;
'If I am good, I'll have a doll
    From Santa Claus'—laughed Emily.

The little ones are gone to sleep,
    Their father and their mother now
Are coming home, with many more—
    They're drunk, and make a merry row.

The little ones on Christmas morn
    Jump up, like skylarks from the grass;
And then they stand as still as stones,
    And just as cold as stones, Alas!

No horse, no doll beside their bed,
  No sadder little ones could be;
'We did some wrong,' said little Will—
  'We must have sinned,' sobbed Emily.

The Sleepers

As I walked down the waterside
  This silent morning, wet and dark;
Before the cocks in farmyards crowed,
  Before the dogs began to bark;
Before the hour of five was struck
By old Westminster's mighty clock:

As I walked down the waterside
  This morning, in the cold damp air,
I saw a hundred women and men
  Huddled in rags and sleeping there:
These people have no work, thought I,
And long before their time they die.

That moment, on the waterside,
  A lighted car came at a bound;
I looked inside, and saw a score
  Of pale and weary men that frowned;
Each man sat in a huddled heap,
Carried to work while fast asleep.

Ten cars rushed down the waterside
  Like lighted coffins in the dark;
With twenty dead men in each car,
  That must be brought alive by work:
These people work too hard, thought I,
And long before their time they die.

The Bed-sitting-room

Must I live here, with Scripture on my walls,
Death-cards with rocks and anchors; on my shelf
Plain men and women with plain histories
A proud landlady knows, and no one else?
Let me have pictures of a richer kind:
Scenes in low taverns, with their beggar rogues
Singing and drinking ale; who buy more joy
With a few pence than others can with pounds.
Show gipsies on wild commons, camped at fires
Close to their caravans; where they cook flesh
They have not bought, and plants not sold to them
Show me the picture of a drinking monk
With his round belly like a mare in foal,
Belted, to keep his guts from falling out
When he laughs hearty; or a maid's bare back,
Who teases me with a bewitching smile
Thrown over her white shoulder. Let me see
The picture of a sleeping damosel,
Who has a stream of shining hair to fill
Up that deep channel banked by her white breasts.
Has Beauty never smiled from off these walls,
Has Genius never entered in a book?
Nay, Madam, keep your room; for in my box
I have a lovely picture of young Eve,
Before she knew what sewing was. Alas!
If I hung on your wall her naked form,
Among your graves and crosses, Scripture texts,
Your death-cards with their anchors and their rocks—
What then? I think this life a joyful thing,
And, like a bird that sees a sleeping cat,
I leave with haste your death-preparing room.

The Child and the Mariner

A dear[23] old couple my grandparents were,
And kind to all dumb things; they saw in Heaven
The lamb that Jesus petted when a child:
Their faith was never draped by Doubt: to them
Death was a rainbow in Eternity,
That promised everlasting brightness soon.
An old seafaring man was he; a rough
Old man, but kind; and hairy, like the nut
Full of sweet milk. All day on shore he watched
The winds for sailors' wives, and told what ships
Enjoyed fair weather, and what ships had storms;
He watched the sky, and he could tell for sure
What afternoons would follow stormy morns,
If quiet nights would end wild afternoons.
He leapt away from scandal with a roar,
And if a whisper still possessed his mind,
He walked about and cursed it for a plague.
He took offence at Heaven when beggars passed,
And sternly called them back to give them help.
In this old captain's house I lived, and things
That house contained were in ships' cabins once;
Sea-shells and charts and pebbles, model ships;
Green weeds, dried fishes stuffed, and coral stalks;
Old wooden trunks with handles of spliced rope,
With copper saucers full of monies strange,
That seemed the savings of dead men, not touched
To keep them warm since their real owners died;
Strings of red beads, methought were dipped in blood,
And swinging lamps, as though the house might move;
An ivory lighthouse built on ivory rocks,
The bones of fishes and three bottled ships.
And many a thing was there which sailors make
In idle hours, when on long voyages,
Of marvellous patience, to no lovely end.

[23] dear [Dear 1911]

And on those charts I saw the small black dots
That were called islands, and I knew they had
Turtles and palms, and pirates' buried gold.
There came a stranger to my grandad's house,
The old man's nephew, a seafarer too;
A big, strong able man who could have walked
Twm Barlum's hill all clad in iron mail;
So strong he could have made one man his club
To knock down others—Henry was his name,
No other name was uttered by his kin.
And here he was, in sooth ill-clad, but oh,
Thought I, what secrets of the sea are his!
This man knows coral islands in the sea,
And dusky girls heart-broken for white men;
This sailor knows of wondrous lands afar,
More rich than Spain, when the Phoenicians shipped
Silver for common ballast, and they saw
Horses at silver mangers eating grain;
This man has seen the wind blow up a mermaid's hair
Which, like a golden serpent, reared and stretched
To feel the air away beyond her head.
He begged my pennies, which I gave with joy—
He will most certainly return some time
A self-made king of some new land, and rich.
Alas that he, the hero of my dreams,
Should be his people's scorn; for they had rose
To proud command of ships, whilst he had toiled
Before the mast for years, and well content;
Him they despised, and only Death could bring
A likeness in his face to show like them.
For he drank all his pay, nor went to sea
As long as ale was easy got on shore.
Now, in his last long voyage he had sailed
From Plymouth Sound to where sweet odours fan
The Cingalese at work, and then back home—
But came not near his kin till pay was spent.
He was not old, yet seemed so; for his face

Looked like the drowned man's in the morgue, when it
Has struck the wooden wharves and keels of ships.
And all his flesh was pricked with Indian ink,
His body marked as rare and delicate
As dead men struck by lightning under trees,
And pictured with fine twigs and curlèd ferns;
Chains on his neck and anchors on his arms;
Rings on his fingers, bracelets on his wrist;
And on his breast the *Jane* of Appledore
Was schooner rigged, and in full sail at sea.
He could not whisper with his strong hoarse voice,
No more than could a horse creep quietly;
He laughed to scorn the men that muffled close
For fear of wind, till all their neck was hid,
Like Indian corn wrapped up in long green leaves;
He knew no flowers but seaweeds brown and green,
He knew no birds but those that followed ships.
Full well he knew the water-world; he heard
A grander music there than we on land,
When organ shakes a church; swore he would make
The sea his home, though it was always roused
By such wild storms as never leave Cape Horn;
Happy to hear the tempest grunt and squeal
Like pigs heard dying in a slaughter-house.
A true-born mariner, and this his hope—
His coffin would be what his cradle was,
A boat to drown in and be sunk at sea;
To drown at sea and lie a dainty corpse
Salted and iced in Neptune's larder deep.
This man despised small coasters, fishing-smacks,
He scorned those sailors who at night and morn
Can see the coast, when in their little boats
They go a six days' voyage and are back
Home with their wives for every Sabbath day.
Much did he talk of tankards of old beer,
And bottled stuff he drank in other lands,
Which was a liquid fire like Hell to gulp,

But Paradise to sip.
                    And so he talked;
Nor did those people listen with more awe
To Lazarus—whom they had seen stone-dead—
Than did we urchins to that seaman's voice.
He many a tale of wonder told: of where,
At Argostoli, Cephalonia's sea
Ran over the earth's lip in heavy floods;
And then again of how the strange Chinese
Conversed much as our homely Blackbirds sing.
He told us how he sailed in one old ship
Near that volcano Martinique, whose power
Shook like dry leaves the whole Caribbean seas;
And made the Sun set in a sea of fire
Which only half was his; and dust was thick
On deck, and stones were pelted at the mast.
So, as we walked along, that seaman dropped
Into my greedy ears such words that sleep
Stood at my pillow half the night perplexed.
He told how isles sprang up and sank again,
Between short voyages, to his amaze;
How they did come and go, and cheated charts;
Told how a crew was cursed when one man killed
A bird that perched upon a moving barque;
And how the sea's sharp needles, firm and strong,
Ripped open the bellies of big, iron ships;
Of mighty icebergs in the Northern seas,
That haunt the far horizon like white ghosts.
He told of waves that lift a ship so high
That birds could pass from starboard unto port
Under her dripping keel.
                    Oh, it was sweet
To hear that seaman tell such wondrous tales:
How deep the sea in parts, that drowned men
Must go a long way to their graves and sink
Day after day, and wander with the tides.
He spake of his own deeds; of how he sailed

One summer's night along the Bosphorus,
And he—who knew no music like the wash
Of waves against a ship, or wind in shrouds—
Heard then the music on that woody shore
Of nightingales, and feared to leave the deck,
He thought 'twas sailing into Paradise.
To hear these stories all we urchins placed
Our pennies in that seaman's ready hand;
Until one morn he signed for a long cruise,
And sailed away—we never saw him more.
Could such a man sink in the sea unknown?
Nay, he had found a land with something rich,
That kept his eyes turned inland for his life.
'A damn bad sailor and a landshark too,
No good in port or out'—my grandad said.

Thunderstorms

My mind has thunderstorms,
    That brood for heavy hours:
Until they rain me words,
    My thoughts are drooping flowers
And sulking, silent birds.

Yet come, dark thunderstorms,
    And brood your heavy hours;
For when you rain me words,
    My thoughts are dancing flowers
And joyful singing birds.

Strong Moments

Sometimes I hear fine ladies sing,
   Sometimes I smoke and drink with men;
Sometimes I play at games of cards—
   Judge me to be no strong man then.

The strongest moment of my life
   Is when I think about the poor;
When, like a spring that rain has fed,
   My pity rises more and more.

The flower that loves the warmth and light
   Has all its mornings bathed in dew;
My heart has moments wet with tears,
   My weakness is they are so few.

A Greeting

Good morning, Life—and all
Things glad and beautiful.
My pockets nothing hold,
But he that owns the gold,
The Sun, is my great friend—
His spending has no end.

Hail to the morning sky,
Which bright clouds measure high;
Hail to you birds whose throats
Would number leaves by notes;
Hail to you shady bowers,
And you green fields of flowers.

Hail to you women fair,
That make a show so rare
In cloth as white as milk—
Be't calico or silk:
Good morning, Life—and all
Things glad and beautiful.

Sweet Stay-at-Home

Sweet Stay-at-Home, sweet Well-content,
Thou knowest of no strange continent:
Thou hast not felt thy bosom keep
A gentle motion with the deep;
Thou hast not sailed in Indian seas,
Where scent comes forth in every breeze.
Thou hast not seen the rich grape grow
For miles, as far as eyes can go;
Thou hast not seen a summer's night
When maids could sew by a worm's light;
Nor the North Sea in spring send out
Bright hues that like birds flit about
In solid cages of white ice—
Sweet Stay-at-Home, sweet Love-one-place.
Thou hast not seen black fingers pick
White cotton when the bloom is thick,
Nor heard black throats in harmony;
Nor hast thou sat on stones that lie
Flat on the earth, that once did rise
To hide proud kings from common eyes;
Thou hast not seen plains full of bloom
Where green things had such little room
They pleased the eye like fairer flowers—
Sweet Stay-at-Home, all these long hours.
Sweet Well-content, sweet Love-one-place,
Sweet, simple maid, bless thy dear face;

For thou hast made more homely stuff
Nurture thy gentle self enough;
I love thee for a heart that's kind—
Not for the knowledge in thy mind.

Christmas

Christmas has come, let's eat and drink—
This is no time to sit and think;
Farewell to study, books and pen,
And welcome to all kinds of men.
Let all men now get rid of care,
And what one has let others share;
Then 'tis the same, no matter which
Of us is poor, or which is rich.
Let each man have enough this day,
Since those that can are glad to pay;
There's nothing now too rich or good
For poor men, not the King's own food.
Now like a singing bird my feet
Touch earth, and I must drink and eat.
Welcome to all men: I'll not care
What any of my fellows wear;
We'll not let cloth divide our souls,
They'll swim stark naked in the bowls.
Welcome, poor beggar: I'll not see
That hand of yours dislodge a flea,—
While you sit at my side and beg,
Or right foot scratching your left leg.
Farewell restraint: we will not now
Measure the ale our brains allow,
But drink as much as we can hold.
We'll count no change when we spend gold;
This is no time to save, but spend,
To give for nothing, not to lend.

Let foes make friends: let them forget
The mischief-making dead that fret
The living with complaint like this—
'He wronged us once, hate him and his.'
Christmas has come; let every man
Eat, drink, be merry all he can.
Ale's my best mark, but if port wine
Or whisky's yours—let it be mine;
No matter what lies in the bowls,
We'll make it rich with our own souls.
Farewell to study, books and pen,
And welcome to all kinds of men.

The Old Oak Tree

I sit beneath your leaves, old oak,
    You mighty one of all the trees;
Within whose hollow trunk a man
    Could stable his big horse with ease.

I see your knuckles hard and strong,
    But have no fear they'll come to blows;
Your life is long, and mine is short,
    But which has known the greater woes?

Thou hast not seen starved women here,
    Or man gone mad because ill-fed—
Who stares at stones in city streets,
    Mistaking them for hunks of bread.

Thou hast not felt the shivering backs
    Of homeless children lying down
And sleeping in the cold, night air—
    Like doors and walls, in London town.

Knowing thou hast not known such shame,
   And only storms have come thy way,
Methinks I could in comfort spend
   My summer with thee, day by day.

To lie by day in thy green shade,
   And in thy hollow rest at night;
And through the open doorway see
   The stars turn over leaves of light.

Poor Kings

God's pity on poor kings,
   They know no gentle rest;
The North and South cry out,
   Cries come from East and West—
'Come, open this new Dock,
   Building, Bazaar, or Fair.'
Lord, what a wretched life
   Such men must bear.

They're followed, watched and spied,
   No liberty they know;
Some eye will watch them still,
   No matter where they go.
When in green lanes I muse,
   Alone, and hear birds sing,
God's pity then, say I,
   On some poor king.

My Youth

My youth was my old age,
    Weary and long;
It had too many cares
    To think of song;
My moulting days all came
    When I was young.

Now, in life's prime, my soul
    Comes out in flower;
Late, as with Robin, comes
    My singing power;
I was not born to joy
    Till this late hour.

Mad Poll

There goes mad Poll, dressed in wild flowers,
    Poor, crazy Poll, now old and wan;
Her hair all down, like any child:
    She swings her two arms like a man.

Poor, crazy Poll is never sad,
    She never misses one that dies;
When neighbours show their new-born babes,
    They seem familiar to her eyes.

Her bonnet's always in her hand,
    Or on the ground, and lying near;
She thinks it is a thing for play,
    Or pretty show, and not to wear.

She gives the sick no sympathy,
    She never soothes a child that cries;
She never whimpers, night or day,
    She makes no moans, she makes no sighs.

She talks about some battle old,
    Fought many a day from yesterday;
And when that war is done, her love—
    'Ha, ha!' Poll laughs, and skips away.

Francis Thompson

Thou hadst no home, and thou couldst see
    In every street the windows' light:
    Dragging thy limbs about all night,
No window kept a light for thee.

However much thou wert distressed,
    Or tired of moving, and felt sick,
    Thy life was on the open deck—
Thou hadst no cabin for thy rest.

Thy barque was helpless 'neath the sky,
    No pilot thought thee worth his pains
    To guide for love or money gains—
Like phantom ships the rich sailed by.

Thy shadow mocked thee night and day,
    Thy life's companion, it alone;
    It did not sigh, it did not moan,
But mocked thy moves in every way.

In spite of all, the mind had force,
    And, like a stream whose surface flows
    The wrong way when a strong wind blows,
It underneath maintained its course.

Oft didst thou think thy mind would flower
    Too late for good, as some bruised tree
    That blooms in Autumn, and we see
Fruit not worth picking, hard and sour.

Some poets *feign* their wounds and scars:
    If they had known real suffering hours,
    They'd show, in place of Fancy's flowers,
More of Imagination's stars.

So, if thy fruits of Poesy
    Are rich, it is at this dear cost—
    That they were nipt by Sorrow's frost,
In nights of homeless misery.

Heigh Ho, the Rain

The Lark that in heaven dim
    Can match a rainy hour
    With his own music's shower,
Can make me sing like him—
    Heigh ho! The rain!

Sing—when a Nightingale
    Pours forth her own sweet soul
    To hear dread thunder roll
Into a tearful tale—
    Heigh ho! The rain!

Sing—when a Sparrow's seen
    Trying to lie at rest
    By pressing his warm breast
To leaves so wet and green—
    Heigh ho! The rain!

Night Wanderers

They hear the bell of midnight toll,
And shiver in their flesh and soul;
They lie on hard, cold wood or stone,

Iron, and ache in every bone;
They hate the night: they see no eyes
Of loved ones in the starlit skies.
They see the cold, dark water near;
They dare not take long looks for fear
They'll fall like those poor birds that see
A snake's eyes staring at their tree.
Some of them laugh, half-mad; and some
All through the chilly night are dumb;
Like poor, weak infants some converse,
And cough like giants, deep and hoarse.

The Two Lives

Now how could I, with gold to spare,
    Who know the harlot's arms, and wine,
Sit in this green field all alone,
    If Nature was not truly mine?

That Pleasure life wakes stale at morn,
    From heavy sleep that no rest brings:
This life of quiet joy wakes fresh,
    And claps its wings at morn, and sings.

So here sit I, alone till noon,
    In one long dream of quiet bliss;
I hear the lark and share his joy,
    With no more winedrops than were his.

Such, Nature, is thy charm and power—
    Since I have made the Muse my wife—
To keep me from the harlot's arms,
    And save me from a drunkard's life.

The Fog

I saw the fog grow thick,
   Which soon made blind my ken;
It made tall men of boys,
   And giants of tall men.

It clutched my throat, I coughed;
   Nothing was in my head
Except two heavy eyes
   Like balls of burning lead.

And when it grew so black
   That I could know no place,
I lost all judgment then,
   Of distance and of space.

The street lamps, and the lights
   Upon the halted cars,
Could either be on earth
   Or be the heavenly stars.

A man passed by me close,
   I asked my way, he said,
'Come, follow me, my friend'—
   I followed where he led.

He rapped the stones in front,
   'Trust me,' he said, 'and come';
I followed like a child—
   A blind man led me home.

Dreams of the Sea

I know not why I yearn for thee again,
   To sail once more upon thy fickle flood;
I'll hear thy waves wash under my death-bed,
   Thy salt is lodged for ever in my blood.

Yet I have seen thee lash the vessel's sides
   In fury, with thy many tailèd whip;
And I have seen thee, too, like Galilee,
   When Jesus walked in peace to Simon's ship.

And I have seen thy gentle breeze as soft
   As summer's, when it makes the cornfields run;
And I have seen thy rude and lusty gale
   Make ships show half their bellies to the sun.

Thou knowest the way to tame the wildest life,
   Thou knowest the way to bend the great and proud:
I think of that Armada whose puffed sails,
   Greedy and large, came swallowing every cloud.

But I have seen the sea-boy, young and drowned,
   Lying on shore and, by thy cruel hand,
A seaweed beard was on his tender chin,
   His heaven-blue eyes were filled with common sand.

And yet, for all, I yearn for thee again,
   To sail once more upon thy fickle flood:
I'll hear thy waves wash under my death-bed,
   Thy salt is lodged for ever in my blood.

The Best Friend

Now shall I walk,
  Or shall I ride?
'Ride,' Pleasure said;
  'Walk,' Joy replied.

Now what shall I—
  Stay home or roam?
'Roam,' Pleasure said;
  And Joy—'Stay home.'

Now shall I dance,
  Or sit for dreams?
'Sit,' answers Joy;
  'Dance,' Pleasure screams.

Which of ye two
  Will kindest be?
Pleasure laughed sweet,
  But Joy kissed me.

Heaven

That paradise the Arab dreams,
Is far less sand and more fresh streams.
The only heaven an Indian knows,
Is hunting deer and buffaloes.
The Yankee heaven—to bring Fame forth
By some freak show of what he's worth.
The heaven that fills an English heart,
Is Union Jacks in every part.
The Irish heaven is heaven of old,
When Satan cracked skulls manifold.

The Scotsman has his heaven to come—
To argue his Creator dumb.
The Welshman's heaven is singing airs—
No matter who feels sick and swears.

The Mind's Liberty

The mind, with its own eyes and ears,
    May for these others have no care;
No matter where this body is,
    The mind is free to go elsewhere.
My mind can be a sailor, when
    This body's still confined to land;
And turn these mortals into trees,
    That walk in Fleet Street or the Strand.

So, when I'm passing Charing Cross,
    Where porters work both night and day,
I ofttimes hear sweet Malpas Brook,
    That flows thrice fifty miles away.
And when I'm passing near St. Paul's,
    I see, beyond the dome and crowd,
Twm Barlum, that green pap in Gwent,
    With its dark nipple in a cloud.

The Weeping Child

What makes thee weep so, little child,
    What cause hast thou for all this grief?
When thou art old much cause may be,
    And tears will bring thee no relief.

Thou dost not know thy mother yet,
    Thou'dst sleep on any bosom near;
Thou dost not see a daughter dying,
    No son is coughing in thy ear.

Thy father is a bearded man,
    Yet any bearded man could take
Thee in his arms, and thou not know
    Which man would die for thy sweet sake.

What makes thee weep then, little child,
    What cause hast thou for all this bother;
Whose father could be any man,
    And any woman be thy mother?

A Fleeting Passion

Thou shalt not laugh, thou shalt not romp,
    Let's grimly kiss with bated breath;
As quietly and solemnly
    As Life when it is kissing Death.
Now in the silence of the grave,
    My hand is squeezing that soft breast;
While thou dost in such passion lie,
    It mocks me with its look of rest.

But when the morning comes at last,
    And we must part, our passions cold,
You'll think of some new feather, scarf
    To buy with my small piece of gold;
And I'll be dreaming of green lanes,
    Where little things with beating hearts
Hold shining eyes between the leaves,
    Till men with horses pass, and carts.

The Hawk

Thou dost not fly, thou art not perched,
    The air is all around:
What is it that can keep thee set,
    From falling to the ground?
The concentration of thy mind
    Supports thee in the air;
As thou dost watch the small young birds,
    With such a deadly care.

My mind has such a hawk as thou,
    It is an evil mood;
It comes when there's no cause for grief,
    And on my joys doth brood.
Then do I see my life in parts;
    The earth receives my bones,
The common air absorbs my mind—
    It knows not flowers from stones.

The Moon

Thy beauty haunts me heart and soul,
    Oh thou fair Moon, so close and bright;
Thy beauty makes me like the child,
    That cries aloud to own thy light:
The little child that lifts each arm,
To press thee to her bosom warm.

Though there are birds that sing this night
    With thy white beams across their throats,
Let my deep silence speak for me
    More than for them their sweetest notes:
Who worships thee till music fails,
Is greater than thy nightingales.

A Great Time

Sweet Chance, that led my steps abroad,
   Beyond the town, where wild flowers grow—
A rainbow and a cuckoo, Lord,
   How rich and great the times are now!
     Know, all ye sheep
     And cows, that keep
On staring that I stand so long
   In grass that's wet from heavy rain—
A rainbow and a cuckoo's song
   May never come together again;
     May never come
     This side the tomb.

The Black Cloud

Little flocks of peaceful clouds,
   Lying in your fields so blue,
While my eyes look up they see
   A black Ram coming close to you.

He will scatter you poor flocks,
   He will tear up north and south;
Lightning will come from his eye,
   And fierce thunder from his mouth.

Little flocks of peaceful clouds,
   Soon there'll be a dreadful rout,
That Ram's horns can toss big ships,
   Tear an oak tree's bowels out.

Rich Days

Welcome to you rich Autumn days,
   Ere comes the cold, leaf-picking wind,
When golden stooks are seen in fields,
   All standing arm-in-arm entwined;
And gallons of sweet cider seen
On trees in apples red and green.

With mellow pears that cheat our teeth,
   Which melt that tongues may suck them in;
With blue-black damsons, yellow plums,[24]
   Now sweet and soft from stone to skin;
And woodnuts rich, to make us go
Into the loneliest[25] lanes we know.

The Child Chatters

Good morning to my dolly first,
   Good morning to my cherry tree;
Good morning to my little chicks,
   For them I love to see.

Good morning to my bow-wow-wow;
   Good morning to my bonnet new;
Good morning to my little self,
   To Dad and Mammie too.

Good morning, God which art in Heaven,
   I hope you slept last night quite well;
And please don't vex your head so much
   About the devil in hell.

[24] With . . . plums, [With cherries red, and blue-black plums, 1914, 1928, 1934]
[25] loneliest [loveliest 1914]

And if he bothers you too much,
     And you're afraid, and you sleep bad,
Then, God which art in Heaven, you must
     Have whisky, like my Dad.

The Hermit

What moves that lonely man is not the boom
     Of waves that break against the cliff so strong;
Nor roar of thunder, when that travelling voice
     Is caught by rocks that carry far along.

'Tis not the groan of oak tree in its prime,
     When lightning strikes its solid heart to dust;
Nor frozen pond when, melted by the sun,
     It suddenly doth break its sparkling crust.

What moves that man is when the blind bat taps
     His window when he sits alone at night;
Or when the small bird sounds like some great beast
     Among the dead, dry leaves so frail and light;

Or when the moths on his night-pillow beat
     Such heavy blows he fears they'll break his bones;
Or when a mouse inside the papered walls,
     Comes like a tiger crunching through the stones.

The Collier's Wife

The collier's wife had four tall sons
     Brought from the pit's mouth dead,
     And crushed from foot to head;
When others brought her husband home,
Had five dead bodies in her room.

91

Had five dead bodies in her house—
    All in a row they lay—
    To bury in one day:
Such sorrow in the valley has
Made kindness grow like grass.

Oh, collier, collier, underground,
    In fear of fire and gas,
    What life more danger has?
Who fears more danger in this life?
There is but one—thy wife!

Stars

One night I saw ten stars take wing—
    Like flowers to butterflies—and fly;
Then I lay down to sleep, a child,
    Though when I woke a man was I.

But when I saw the stars again,
    So steadfast in their heavenly home;
The same ten thousand years ago,
    The same ten thousand years to come—

Methought, what are they laughing at—
    How close our cradles are to graves?
Do they, in their eternal pride,
    Make merry at our little lives?

And sure, the Moon was laughing too;
    The great, white Moon, that I could see
Shaking her sides, low in the west,
    Like a big rattle in a tree.

Come, Let Me Close

Come, let me close thine eyes with kisses—
  And those two lips that day and night
Are opened to a cherry's size,
  And cry for Love to kiss them tight.
Let me enjoy thy bosom now,
  Sweet Lady, let my head rock there;
When it is wedged between thy breasts,
  Throw over it thy silken hair.

Let me lie close before He comes
  To clasp thy bosom like a leech:
I mean that babe, who'll lie between,
  Over whose body I must reach;
That tyrant babe, whom thou wilt love
  Above all earthly things the best:
Though laughing he will trample, kick
  And knuckle into each soft breast.

On the Mountain

When from this mighty mountain's top
  My wandering eyes go forth,
Trees look like bonnets, fields like flags
  In all those miles of earth.
I see afar big towns look now
  Like flocks of sheep washed white;
And villages—their straggling lambs—
  May never meet my sight.

Windows—no more than drops of dew—
  Are sparkling in the green;
The sun in heaven seems small indeed,
  To light so vast a scene.

A mighty stretch of land like this,
    Doth make me shut my eyes;
For when I look I fear to see
    Its sudden fall or rise.

The Rev. Ebenezer Paul

He begs from rich men for the poor,
    And robs the poor of Christmas dinners.
Ah, cruel Time, to keep alive
    For all these years such hoary sinners!
This hard, old man with silvery locks,
    With false, white teeth—see how he fawns!
Feel in that hair, and I'll be damned
    If thou'lt not find the Devil's horns!

This stack of infamy, that keeps
    Dark, greedy thoughts like rats within;
This stack that harbours gentle looks,
    Like snakes with their cold, smiling skin;
This gospel-monger, old and bland,
    Who prays aloud for other sinners—
He begs from rich men for the poor,
    And robs the poor of Christmas dinners.

Nell Barnes

They lived apart for three long years,
    Bill Barnes and Nell, his wife;
He took his joy from other girls,
    She led a wicked life.

Yet ofttimes she would pass his shop,
   With some strange man awhile;
And, looking, meet her husband's frown
   With her malicious smile.

Until one day, when passing there,
   She saw her man had gone;
And when she saw the empty shop,
   She fell down with a moan.

And when she heard that he had gone
   Five thousand miles away,
And that she'd see his face no more,
   She sickened from that day.

To see his face was health and life,
   And when it was denied,
She could not eat, and broke her heart—
   It was for love she died.

The Bird of Paradise

Here comes Kate Summers who, for gold,
   Takes any man to bed:
'You knew my friend, Nell Barnes,' said she;
   'You knew Nell Barnes—she's dead.

'Nell Barnes was bad on all you men,
   Unclean, a thief as well;
Yet all my life I have not found
   A better friend than Nell.

'So I sat at her side at last,
   For hours, till she was dead;
And yet she had no sense at all
   Of any word I said.

'For all her cry but came to this—
    "Not for the world! Take care:
Don't touch that bird of paradise,
    Perched on the bedpost there!"

'I asked her would she like some grapes,
    Some damsons ripe and sweet;
A custard made with new-laid eggs,
    Or tender fowl to eat.

'I promised I would follow her,
    To see her in her grave;
And buy a wreath with borrowed pence,
    If nothing I could save.

'Yet still her cry but came to this—
    "Not for the world! Take care:
Don't touch that bird of paradise,
    Perched on the bedpost there!" '

This Night

This night, as I sit here alone,
And brood on what is dead and gone,
The owl that's in this Highgate Wood
Has found his fellow in my mood;
To every star, as it doth rise—
Oh-o-o! Oh-o-o! he shivering cries.

And, looking at the Moon this night,
There's that dark shadow in her light.
Ah! Life and Death, my fairest one,
Thy lover is a skeleton!
'And why is that?' I question—'why?'
Oh-o-o! oh-o-o! the owl doth cry.

Kitty and I

The gentle wind that waves
   The green boughs here and there,
Is showing how my hand
   Waved Kitty's finer hair.

The Bee, when all his joints
   Are clinging to a Blossom,
Is showing how I clung
   To Kitty's softer bosom.

The Rill, when his sweet voice
   Is hushed by water-cresses,
Is Kitty's sweeter voice
   Subdued by my long kisses.

Those little stars that shine
   So happy in the skies,
Are those sweet babes I saw,
   Whose heaven was Kitty's eyes.

The Moon, that casts her beam
   Upon the hill's dark crest,
Is Kitty's whiter arm
   Across my hairy breast.

The hazel nuts, when paired
   Unseen beneath the boughs,
Are Kitty and myself,
   Whenever Chance allows.

Thou Comest, May

Thou comest, May, with leaves and flowers,
  And nights grow short, and days grow long;
And for thy sake in bush and tree,
  The small birds sing, both old and young;
And only I am dumb and wait
The passing of a fish-like state.

You birds, you old grandfathers now,
  That have such power to welcome spring,
I, but a father in my years,
  Have nothing in my mind to sing;
My lips, like gills in deep-sea homes,
Beat time, and still no music comes.

The Hospital Waiting-Room

We wait our turn, as still as mice,
For medicine free, and free advice:
Two mothers, and their little girls
So small—each one with flaxen curls—
And I myself, the last to come.
Now as I entered that bare room,
I was not seen or heard; for both
The mothers—one in finest cloth,
With velvet blouse and crocheted lace,
Lips painted red, and powdered face;
The other ragged, whose face took
Its own dull, white, and wormy look—
Exchanged a hard and bitter stare.
And both the children, sitting there,
Taking example from that sight,
Made ugly faces, full of spite.
This woman said, though not a word
From her red painted lips was heard—

'Why have I come to this, to be
In such a slattern's company?'
The ragged woman's look replied—
'If you can dress with so much pride,
Why are you here, so neat, and nice,
For medicine free, and free advice?'
And I, who needed richer food,
Not medicine, to help my blood;
Who could have swallowed then a horse,
And chased its rider round the course,
Sat looking on, ashamed, perplexed,
Until a welcome voice cried—'Next!'

The White Cascade

What happy mortal sees that mountain now,
The white cascade that's shining on its brow;

The white cascade that's both a bird and star,
That has a ten-mile voice and shines as far?

Though I may never leave this land again,
Yet every spring my mind must cross the main

To hear and see that water-bird and star
That on the mountain sings, and shines so far.

The Inquest

I took my oath I would inquire,
    Without affection, hate, or wrath,
Into the death of Ada Wright—
    So help me God! I took that oath.

When I went out to see the corpse,
    The four months' babe that died so young,
I judged it was seven pounds in weight,
    And little more than one foot long.

One eye, that had a yellow lid,
    Was shut—so was the mouth, that smiled;
The left eye open, shining bright—
    It seemed a knowing little child.

For as I looked at that one eye,
    It seemed to laugh, and say with glee:
'What caused my death you'll never know—
    Perhaps my mother murdered me.'

When I went into court again,
    To hear the mother's evidence—
It was a love-child, she explained.
    And smiled, for our intelligence.

'Now, Gentlemen of the Jury,' said
    The coroner—'this woman's child
By misadventure met its death.'
    'Aye, aye,' said we. The mother smiled.

And I could see that child's one eye
    Which seemed to laugh, and say with glee:
'What caused my death you'll never know—
    Perhaps my mother murdered me.'

The Two Children

    'Ah, little boy! I see
        You have a wooden spade.
    Into this sand you dig
        So deep—for what?' I said.

100

'There's more rich gold,' said he,
    'Down under where I stand,
Than twenty elephants
    Could move across the land.'

'Ah, little girl with wool!—
    What are you making now?'
'Some stockings for a bird,
    To keep his legs from snow.'
And there those children are,
    So happy, small, and proud:
The boy that digs his grave,
    The girl that knits her shroud.

Come, thou Sweet Wonder

Come, thou sweet Wonder, by whose power
    We more or less enjoy our years;
That mak'st a child forget the breast,
    And dry'st at once the children's tears,
Till sleep shall bring their minds more rest.

Come to my heavy rain of care,
    And make it weigh like dew; charm me
With Beauty's hair, her eyes or lips;
    With mountain dawn, or sunset sea
That's like a thousand burning ships.

Charms

She walks as lightly as the fly
Skates on the water in July.

To hear her moving petticoat,
For me is music's highest note.

Stones are not heard, when her feet pass,
No more than tumps of moss or grass.

When she sits still, she's like the flower
To be a butterfly next hour.

The brook laughs not more sweet, when he
Trips over pebbles suddenly.

My Love, like him, can whisper low—
When he comes where green cresses grow.

She rises like the lark, that hour
He goes half-way to meet a shower.

A fresher drink is in her looks
Than Nature gives me, or old books.

When I in my Love's shadow sit,
I do not miss the sun one bit.

When she is near, my arms can hold
All that's worth having in this world.

And when I know not where she is,
Nothing can come but comes amiss.

Friends

They're creeping on the stairs outside,
    They're whispering soft and low;
Now up, now down, I hear his friends,
    And still they come and go.

The sweat that runs my side, from that
    Hot pit beneath my shoulder,
Is not so cold as he will be,
    Before the night's much older.

My fire I feed with naked hands,
    No sound shall reach their ears;
I'm moving like the careful cat,
    That stalks a rat it fears.

And as his friends still come and go,
    A thoughtful head is mine:
Had Life as many friends as Death,
    Lord, how this world would shine!

And since I'll have so many friends,
    When on my death-bed lying—
I wish my life had more love now,
    And less when I am dying.

The Power of Silence

And will she never hold her tongue,
    About that feather in her hat;
    Her scarf, when she has done with that,
And then the bangle on her wrist;
    And is my silence meant to make
Her talk the more—the more she's kissed?

At last, with silence matching mine,
    She feels the passion deep and strong,
    That fears to trust a timid tongue.
Say, Love—that draws us close together—
    Isn't she the very life of Death?
No more of bangle, scarf or feather.

In Neath Valley

    Between two rows of trees,
    Here let me take my ease;

To see the light afar,
Shining like one big star.

It is not fine to lie
With boughs to change my sky;

Alone in this green way,
And let my fancies play?

Now as a growing boy
Will sometimes stand for joy

Tiptoe behind men small,
And raise himself as tall—

So shall my fancy's eye
See none more great than I.

The Blind Boxer

He goes with basket and slow feet,
To sell his nuts from street to street;
The very terror of his kind,
Till blackened eyes had made him blind.
For this is Boxer Bob, the man
That had hard muscles, harder than
A schoolboy's bones; who held his ground
When six tall bullies sparred around.
Small children now, that have no grace,
Can steal his nuts before his face;
And when he threatens with his hands,
Mock him two feet from where he stands;
Mock him who could some years ago
Have leapt five feet to strike a blow.
Poor Bobby, I remember when
Thou wert a god to drunken men;

But now they push thee off, or crack
Thy nuts and give no money back.
They swear they'll strike thee in the face,
Dost thou not hurry from that place.
Such are the men that once would pay
To keep thee drunk from day to day.
With all thy strength and cunning skill,
Thy courage, lasting breath and will,
Thou'rt helpless now; a little ball,
No bigger than a cherry small,
Has now refused to guide and lead
Twelve stone of strong hard flesh that need
But that ball's light to make thee leap
And strike these cowards down like sheep.
Poor helpless Bobby, blind; I see
Thy working face and pity thee.

I am the Poet Davies, William[26]

I am the Poet Davies, William,
    I sin without a blush or blink:
I am a man that lives to eat;
    I am a man that lives to drink.

My face is large, my lips are thick,
    My skin is coarse and black almost;
But the ugliest feature is my verse,
    Which proves my soul is black and lost.

Thank heaven thou didst not marry me,
    A poet full of blackest evil;
For how to manage my damned soul
    Will puzzle many a flaming devil.

[26] I ... William [To the Woman who will read this Poem to her Husband 1918]

The Moon and a Cloud[27]

Sometimes I watch the moon at night,
   No matter be she near or far;
Up high, or in a leafy tree
   Caught laughing like a bigger star.

To-night the west is full of clouds;
   The east is full of stars that fly
Into the cloud's dark foliage,
   And the moon will follow by and by.

I see a dark brown shabby cloud—
   The moon has gone behind its back;
I looked to see her turn it white—
   She turned it to a lovely black.

A lovely cloud, a jet-black cloud;
   It shines with such a glorious light,
That I am glad with all my heart
   She turned it black instead of white.

The Hunt

We have no mind to reach that Pole
   Where monarchs keep their icy courts,
Where lords and ladies, proud and cold,
   May do no more than smile at sports;
Nay, laughing, lying at our ease
We keep our court beneath green trees.

King's beds are soft and silvery white,
   While ours are golden straw or hay:

[27] The . . . Cloud [Wasting Time 1918]

So let kings lie, while gentle sleep
   Attends our harder beds, when they,
Inside their soft white bedclothes, yell
That nightmares ride them down to hell.

Poor lords and ladies, what tame sport
   To hunt a fox or stag, while we
Sit on a green bank in the sun
   And chase for hours a faster flea;
Which blesses us from day to day,
With all our faculties in play.

Confession

One hour in every hundred hours
I sing of childhood, birds and flowers;
Who reads my character in song
Will not see much in me that's wrong.

But in my ninety hours and nine
I would not tell what thoughts are mine:
They're not so pure as find their words
In songs of childhood, flowers and birds.

Easter

What exultations in my mind
From the love-bite of this Easter wind!
My head thrown back, my face doth shine
Like yonder Sun's, but warmer mine.
A butterfly—from who knows where?—
Comes with a stagger through the air,
And, lying down, doth ope and close
His wings, as babies work their toes;

Perhaps he thinks of pressing tight
Into his wings a little light!
And many a bird hops in between
The leaves he dreams of, long and green,
And sings for nipple-buds that show
Where the full-breasted leaves must grow.
Winter is dead, and now we sing
This welcome to the new-born Spring.

My Old Acquaintance

Working her toothless gums till her sharp chin
Could almost reach and touch her sharper nose,
These are the words my old acquaintance said:
'I have four children, all alive and well;
My eldest girl was seventy years in March,
And though when she was born her body was
Covered all over with black hair, and long,
Which when I saw at first made me cry out,
'Take it away, it is a monkey—ugh!'
Yet she's as smooth and fair as any, now.
And I, who sit for hours in this green space
That has seven currents of good air, and pray
At night to Jesus and His Mother, live
In hopes to reach my ninetieth year in June.
But ere it pleases God to take my soul,
I'll sell my fine false teeth, which cost five pounds,
Preserved in water now for twenty years,
For well I know those girls will fight for them
As soon as I am near my death; before
My skin's too cold to feel the feet of flies.
God bless you and good day—I wish you well.
For me, I cannot relish food, or sleep,
Till God sees fit to hold the Kaiser fast,
Stabbed, shot, or hanged—and his black soul
Sent into hell, to bubble, burn and squeal;
Think of the price of fish—and look at bacon!'

A Winter's Night

It is a winter's night and cold,
　The wind is blowing half a gale;
I, with a red-hot poker, stir
　To take the chill off my old ale.

I drink my ale, I smoke my pipe,
　While fire-flames leap to fight the cold;
And yet, before my bedtime comes,
　I must look out on the wide world.

And what strange beauty I behold:
　The wild fast-driven clouds this night
Hurled at the moon, whose smiling face
　Still shines with undiminished light.

The Excuse

'Why did you kill that harmless frog?
　Tell me, my little boy.'
He hung his head for shame, and gone
　Was all his joy.

But now a thought comes to his mind,
　He lifts his head with pride:
'I only *half*-killed it,' he said—
　'And then it died.'

In the Snow

Hear how my friend the robin sings!
　That little hunchback in the snow,
As it comes down as fast as rain.
　The air is cold, the wind doth blow,
And still his heart can feel no pain.

And I, with heart as light as his,
    And to my ankles deep in snow,
Hold up a fist as cold as Death's,
    And into it I laugh and blow—
I laugh and blow my life's warm breath.

Molly

Molly, with hips and ankles plump,
    With hands and feet and waist so small,
Whose breasts could carry flowers unpinned,
    And not one blossom fall—
Give me your answer plain and true,
Do you love me as I love you?

Molly, as timid as a sheep
    That trembles at the shadow
Of any harmless little bird
    That flies across its meadow,
Are you a sweet good-tempered maid?
'Sometimes I'd crush a grape!' she said.

Molly, as gentle as the sun
    That lifts the dew to Heaven's breast,
Of all the lovers you have had,
    Am I the one that's loved the best?
'By all the men betrayed by me,
I swear I love you true,' said she.

Killed in Action
(EDWARD THOMAS)

Happy the man whose home is still
    In Nature's green and peaceful ways;

To wake and hear the birds so loud,
    That scream for joy to see the sun
Is shouldering past a sullen cloud.

And we have known those days, when we
    Would wait to hear the cuckoo first;
When you and I, with thoughtful mind,
    Would help a bird to hide her nest,
For fear of other hands less kind.

But thou, my friend, art lying dead:
    War, with its hell-born childishness,
Has claimed thy life, with many more:
    The man that loved this England well,
And never left it once before.

Cowslips and Larks

I hear it said yon land is poor,
In spite of those rich cowslips there—
And all the singing larks it shoots
To heaven from the cowslips' roots.
But I, with eyes that beauty find,
And music ever in my mind,
Feed my thoughts well upon that grass
Which starves the horse, the ox, and ass.
So here I stand, two miles to come
To Shapwick and my ten-days-home,
Taking my summer's joy, although
The distant clouds are dark and low,
And comes a storm that, fierce and strong,
Has brought the Mendip Hills along:
Those hills that, when the light is there,
Are many a sunny mile from here.

Forgiveness

Stung by a spiteful wasp,
　I let him go life free;
That proved the difference
　In him and me.

For, had I killed my foe,
　It had proved me at once
The stronger wasp, and no
　More difference.

Till I Went Out

Till I went out of doors to prove
What through my window I saw move;
To see if grass was brighter yet,
And if the stones were dark and wet;

Till I went out to see a sign—
That slanted rain, so light and fine,
Had almost settled in my mind
That I at last could see the wind.

The Girl is Mad

She changes oft—she laughs and weeps,
　She smiles, and she can frown;
Should tears of sorrow fill her eyes,
　Then laughter shakes them down:
The girl is mad—and yet I love her.

She smiles, and swears her jealousy
　　Would tear out my two eyes,
And make me swallow them by force:
　　These words are no strong lies,
For she is mad—and yet I love her.

'Ha, ha!' says she; 'I've killed two men,
　　And you're the third I'll kill!'
If I keep time with her fierce love,
　　'Tis certain that she will:
The girl is mad—and yet I love her.

In Time of War

As I go walking down the street
Many's the lad and lass I meet;
There's many a soldier I see pass,
And every soldier has his lass.

But when I saw the others there,
The women that black mourning wear,
'Judged by the looks of these,' I said,
'The lads those lassies court are dead.'

England

We have no grass locked up in ice so fast
That cattle cut their faces and at last,
When it is reached, must lie them down and starve,
With bleeding mouths that freeze too hard to move.[28]
We have not that delirious state of cold
That makes men warm and sing when in Death's hold.
We have no roaring floods whose angry shocks
Can kill the fishes dashed against their rocks.

[28] With . . . move. [Their bleeding mouths being froze too hard to move. 1918]

We have no winds that cut down street by street,
As easy as our scythes can cut down wheat.
No mountains here to spew their burning hearts
Into the valleys, on our human parts.
No earthquakes here, that ring church bells afar,
A hundred miles from where those earthquakes are.
We have no cause to set our dreaming eyes,
Like Arabs, on fresh streams in Paradise.
We have no wilds to harbour men that tell
More murders than they can remember well.
No woman here shall wake from her night's rest,
To find a snake is sucking at her breast.
Though I have travelled many and many a mile,
And had a man to clean my boots and smile
With teeth that had less bone in them than gold—
Give me this England now for all my world.

Note: This poem was included in *Raptures* in May 1918 entitled
In England.

Come, let us Find

Come, let us find a cottage, love,
    That's green for half a mile around;
To laugh at every grumbling bee,
    Whose sweetest blossom's not yet found.
Where many a bird shall sing for you,
    And in our garden build its nest:
They'll sing for you as though their eggs
    Were lying in your breast,
        My love—
    Were lying warm in your soft breast.

'Tis strange how men find time to hate,
    When life is all too short for love;
But we, away from our own kind,
    A different life can live and prove.

And early on a summer's morn,
    As I go walking out with you,
We'll help the sun with our warm breath
    To clear away the dew,
        My love,
    To clear away the morning dew.

The Birds of Steel

This apple-tree, that once was green,
    Is now a thousand flowers in one!
And, with their bags strapped to their thighs,
    There's many a bee that comes for sweets,
To stretch each bag to its full size.

And when the night has grown a moon,
    And I lie half-asleep in bed,
I hear those bees again—ah no,
    It is the birds of steel, instead,
Seeking their innocent prey below.

Man-ridden birds of steel, unseen,
    That come to drop their murdering lime
On any child or harmless thing
    Before the early morning time:
Up, nearer to God, they fly and sing.

The Dancer

The great white Moon is not so fair—
When not one trembling star will dare
To shine within her zone of air.

And lo, this blue-eyed maiden soon
Moves lightly to the music's tune—
Light as a water-fly in June.

As she goes spinning round and round,
Her nimble toes, without a sound,
Sip honey from the common ground.

Like the humming-bird that, swift and strong,
Will never suck but, flying along,
Just lick the blossoms with his tongue.

Dance, dance, thou blue-eyed wonder, dance!
I still believe there's one small chance
Thou'lt fall into my arms in a trance.

On Hearing Mrs. Woodhouse
Play the Harpsichord

We poets pride ourselves on what
    We feel, and not what we achieve;
The world may call our children fools,
    Enough for us that we conceive.
A little wren that loves the grass
Can be as proud as any lark
    That tumbles in a cloudless sky,
Up near the sun, till he becomes
    The apple of that shining eye.

So, lady, I would never dare
    To hear your music ev'ry day;
With those great bursts that send my nerves
    In waves to pound my heart away;
And those small notes that run like mice

Bewitched by light; else on those keys—
    My tombs of song—you should engrave:
'My music, stronger than his own,
    Has made this poet my dumb slave.'

Passion's Greed

His constant wonder keeps him back
    From flying either far or straight;
Confined by thy great beauty here,
    My life is like that butterfly's,
With every source of wonder near.

Let me go burning to my death:
    Nothing can come between our minds
To ease me of this passion's greed:
    We'll bite each other's neck like dogs,
And ask our fingers if we bleed.

Oh, Sweet Content!

Oh, sweet content, that turns the labourer's sweat
    To tears of joy, and shines the roughest face;
How often have I sought you high and low,
    And found you still in some lone quiet place.

Here, in my room, when full of happy dreams,
    With no life heard beyond that merry sound
Of moths that on my lighted ceiling kiss
    Their shadows as they dance and dance around.

Or in a garden, on a summer's night
  When I have seen the dark and solemn air
Blink with the blind bat's wings, and heaven's bright face
  Twitch with the stars that shine in thousands there.

The Villain

While joy gave clouds the light of stars,
  That beamed where'er they looked;
And calves and lambs had tottering knees,
  Excited, while they sucked;
While every bird enjoyed his song,
Without one thought of harm or wrong—
I turned my head and saw the wind,
  Not far from where I stood,
Dragging the corn by her golden hair,
  Into a dark and lonely wood.

The Rat

'That woman there is almost dead,
Her feet and hands like heavy lead;
Her cat's gone out for his delight,
He will not come again this night.

'Her husband in a pothouse drinks,
Her daughter at a soldier winks;
Her son is at his sweetest game,
Teasing the cobbler old and lame.

'Now with these teeth that powder stones,
I'll pick at one of her cheek-bones:
When husband, son and daughter come,
They'll soon see who was left at home.'

The Cat

Within that porch, across the way,
  I see two naked eyes this night;
Two eyes that neither shut nor blink,
  Searching my face with a green light.

But cats to me are strange, so strange—
  I cannot sleep if one is near;
And though I'm sure I see those eyes,
  I'm not so sure a body's there!

To-day

I have no hopes, I have no fears,
Whether my dreams are gossamers
To last beyond my body's day,
Or cobwebs to be brushed away.
Give me this life from hour to hour,
From day to day, and year to year;
This cottage with one extra room
To lodge a friend if he should come;
This garden green and small, where I
Can sit and see a great big sky.
And give me one tall shady tree,
Where, looking through the boughs, I'll see
How the sharp leaves can cut the skies
Into a thousand small blue eyes.

When Leaves Begin

When leaves begin to show their heads,
  Before they reach their curly youth;
And birds in streams are coming north,
  With seas of music from the south;

Then—like a snail with horns outstretched—
My senses feel the air around;
There's not a move escapes my eyes,
My ears are cocked to every sound.

Till Nature to her greenest comes,
And—with her may that blossoms white—
Bursts her full bodice, and reveals
Her fair white body in the light.

Passion's Hounds

With mighty leaps and bounds,
I followed Passion's hounds,
    My hot blood had its day;
Lust, Gluttony, and Drink,
I chased to Hell's black brink,
    Both night and day.

I ate like three strong men,
I drank enough for ten,
    Each hour must have its glass:
Yes, Drink and Gluttony
Have starved more brains, say I,
    Than Hunger has.

And now, when I grow old,
And my slow blood is cold,
    And feeble is my breath—
I'm followed by those hounds,
Whose mighty leaps and bounds
    Hunt me to death.

· The Truth

Since I have seen a bird one day,
· His head pecked more than half away;
That hopped about with but one eye,
Ready to fight again, and die—
Ofttimes since then their private lives
Have spoilt that joy their music gives.

So when I see this robin now,
Like a red apple on the bough,
And question why he sings so strong,
For love, or for the love of song;
Or sings, maybe, for that sweet rill
Whose silver tongue is never still—

Ah, now there comes this thought unkind,
Born of the knowledge in my mind:
He sings in triumph that last night
He killed his father in a fight;
And now he'll take his mother's blood—
The last strong rival for his food.

Love's Caution

Tell them, when you are home again,
    How warm the air was now;
How silent were the birds and leaves,
    And of the moon's full glow;
        And how we saw afar
        A falling star:
It was a tear of pure delight
Ran down the face of Heaven this happy night.

Our kisses are but love in flower,
    Until that greater time
When, gathering strength, those flowers take wing,
    And Love can reach his prime.
      And now, my heart's delight,
      Good night, good night;
Give me the last sweet kiss—
But do not breathe at home one word of this!

A Child's Pet

When I sailed out of Baltimore,
    With twice a thousand head of sheep,
They would not eat, they would not drink,
    But bleated o'er the deep.

Inside the pens we crawled each day,
    To sort the living from the dead;
And when we reached the Mersey's mouth,
    Had lost five hundred head.

Yet every night and day one sheep,
    That had no fear of man or sea,
Stuck through the bars its pleading face,
    And it was stroked by me.

And to the sheep-men standing near,
    'You see,' I said, 'this one tame sheep?
It seems a child has lost her pet,
    And cried herself to sleep.'

So every time we passed it by,
    Sailing to England's slaughter-house,
Eight ragged sheep-men—tramps and thieves—
    Would stroke that sheep's black nose.

One Thing Wanting

'Your life was hard with mangling clothes,
You scrubbed our floors for years;
But now, your children are so good,
That you can rest your poor old limbs,
And want for neither drink nor meat.'
'It's true,' she said, and laughed for joy;
And still her voice, with all her years,
Could make a song-bird wonder if
A rival sweetness challenged him.
But soon her face was full of trouble:
'If I could only tear,' she said,
'My sister Alice out of her grave—
Who taunted me when I was poor—
And make her understand these words:
"See, I have everything I want,
My children, Alice, are so good"—
If I could only once do that,
There's nothing else I want on earth.'

Her Mouth and Mine

As I lay dreaming, open-eyed,
With some one sitting at my side,
I saw a thing about to fly
Into my face, where it would lie;
For just above my head there stood
A smiling hawk as red as blood.
On which the bird, whose quiet nest
Has always been in my left breast,
Seeing that red hawk hovering there,
And smiling with such deadly care—
Flew fascinated to my throat,
And there it moaned a feeble note.

I saw that hawk, so red, and still,
And closed my eyes—it had its will:
For, uttering one triumphant croon,
It pounced with sudden impulse down;
And there I lay, no power to move,
To let it kiss or bite its love.
But in those birds—Ah, it was strange—
There came at last this other change:
That fascinated bird of mine
Worried the hawk and made it whine;
The hawk cried feebly—'Oh dear, oh!
Greedy-in-love, leave go! Leave go!'

from The Song of Life

XIV

I hear men say: 'This Davies has no depth,
He writes of birds, of staring cows and sheep,
And throws no light on deep, eternal things'—
And would they have me talking in my sleep?. . .

XX

Why should this toil from early morn till night
Employ our minds and bodies, when the Earth
Can carry us for ever round the Sun
Without the help of any mortal birth?

XXI

And why should common shelter, bread and meat,
Keep all our faculties in their employ,
And leave no time for ease, while Summer's in
The greenwood, purring like a cat for joy?

XXII

For still the People are no more than slaves;
Each State a slave-ship, and no matter which
The figure-head—a President or King;
The People are no more than common grass
To make a few choice cattle fat and rich.

XXIII

They toil from morn till eve, from Youth to Age;
They go from bud to seed, but never flower.
'Ah,' says the Priest, 'we're born to suffer here
A hell on earth till God Almighty's Hour.'

XXIV

A hell on earth? . . . We'll ask the merry Moth
That, making a partner of his shadow thrown,
Dances till out of breath; we'll ask the Lark
That meets the Rain half-way and sings it down.

XXV

In studying Life we see this human world
Is in three states—of copper, silver, gold,
And those that think in silver take the joy;
Thinking in copper, gold, the poor and rich
Keep mis'ry in too little and too much.

XXVI

Though with my money I could cram a mouth
Big as an Alpine gorge with richest stuff,
Yet Nature sets her bounds; and with a lake
Of wine—to-night one bottle is enough.

XXVII

If I can pluck the rose of sunset, or
The Moon's pale lily, and distil their flower
Into one mental drop to scent my soul—
I'll envy no man his more worldly power.

XXVIII

What matters that my bed is soft and white,
If beggars sleep more sweet in hay, or there,
Lying at noon beneath those swaying boughs
Whose cooling shadows lift the heavy air.

XXIX

Not owning house or land, but in the space
Our minds inhabit, we are rich or poor:
If I had youth, who dances in his walk,
On heels as nimble as his lighter toes,
I'd set no price on any earthly store.

XXX

And wine and women, both have had their day,
When nothing else would my crazed thoughts allow;
Until my nerves shook like those withered leaves
Held by a broken cobweb to the bough . . .

The Hour of Magic

This is the hour of magic, when the Moon
    With her bright wand has charmed the tallest tree
To stand stone-still with all his million leaves!
    I feel around me things I cannot see;
I hold my breath, as Nature holds her own.

And do the mice and birds, the horse and cow,
Sleepless in this deep silence, so intense,
    Believe a miracle has happened now,
And wait to hear a sound they'll recognize,
To prove they still have life with earthly ties?

The Beautiful

Three things there are more beautiful
    Than any man could wish to see:
The first, it is a full-rigged ship
    Sailing with all her sails set free;
The second, when the wind and sun
    Are playing in a field of corn;
The third, a woman, young and fair,
    Showing her child before it is born.

Two Women

The Mother

The midwife nearly drowned my son,
    And beat him hard, before he'd give
That cry a mother longs to hear
    To prove her precious babe will live.

The Wife

I wish that she had drowned him quite,
    Or beat your precious babe to death;
Since he has grown so fierce and strong
    He'll beat me out of my last breath.

Your precious babe is now a man,
    But, mother, he's not worth the skin—
As husband, father, or a son—
    That he was made for living in.

Pastures

That grass is tender, soft and sweet,
    And well you young lambs know't:
I know a pasture twice as sweet,
    Although I may not show't;
Where my five fingers go each night
    To nibble, like you sheep,
All over my love's breast, and there
    Lie down to sleep.

Wild Oats

How slowly moves the snail, that builds
A silver street so fine and long:
I move as slowly, but I leave
Behind me not one breath of song.
Dumb as a moulting bird am I,
I go to bed when children do,
My ale but two half-pints a day,
And to one woman I am true.
Oh! what a life, how flat and stale—
How dull, monotonous and slow!
Can I sing songs in times so dead—
Are there no more wild oats to sow?

A Thought

When I look into a glass,
   Myself's my only care;
But I look into a pool
   For all the wonders there.

When I look into a glass,
   I see a fool:
But I see a wise man
   When I look into a pool.

Strength

What lies I read, that men of strength
Have keen and penetrating looks
That, flashing here and flashing there,
Command success—what foolish books!
For when we go to life we find
The men and dogs that fight till death
Are sleepy-eyed, and look so calm
We wonder if they live by breath!
Love, too, must hold her saucy tongue,
And turn on us two sleepy eyes,
To prove she is no painted doll,
And full, like books, of pretty lies.

To Bacchus

I'm none of those—Oh Bacchus, blush!
   That eat sour pickles with their beer,
To keep their brains and bellies cold;
   Ashamed to let one laughing tear
Escape their hold.

For only just to smell your hops
    Can make me fat and laugh all day,
With appetite for bread and meat:
    I'll not despise bruised apples, they
Make cider sweet.

'Tis true I only eat to live,
    But how I live to drink is clear;
A little isle of meat and bread,
    In one vast sea of foaming beer.
And I'm well fed.

A Woman's History

When Mary Price was five years old,
    And had a bird that died,
She laid its body under flowers;
    And called her friends to pray to God,
And sing sad hymns for hours.

When she, before her fifteenth year,
    Was ruined by a man,
The neighbours sought him out, and said—
    'You'll come along and marry her,
Or hang till you are dead.'

When they had found the child he wronged,
    And playing with her doll,
'I'll come along with you,' said she—
    'But I'll not marry anyone
Unless my doll's with me.'

With no more love's heat in her than
    The wax upon her arm;
With no more love-light in her eyes
    Than in the glass eyes of her doll—
Nor wonder, nor surprise.

When Mary Price was thirty-five,
   And he was lying dead,
She wept as though her heart would break:
   But neighbours winked to see her tears
Fall on a lover's neck.

Now, Mary Price is seventy-five,
   And skinning eels alive:
She, active, strong, and full of breath,
   Has caught the cat that stole an eel,
And beaten it to death.

from The Trance

The Moon is beautiful this night:
She is so clear and bright,
That should she smile
On any sleeping face awhile,
The eyes must then their slumber break,
And open, wide awake;
And should she pass a sleeping bird,
Where no leaves touch or meet,
He'll wake and, in his softest voice,
Cry Sweet! Sweet! Sweet!
The Moon is beautiful, but who is this
That hides his face from hers;
That, when she makes eyes through the leaves,
Is full of trembling fears?
The night breeds many a thing that's strange:
The wretched owl that in distress
Hoots every star that comes to help
The evening in her loveliness;
The half-blind bats that here and there
Are floundering in the twilight air;
The rat, that shows his long white teeth

Of hard, unbreakable bone—
That take him where his notions go,
Through wood and lead, cement and stone;
And cats, that have the power,
About the midnight hour,
To hide their bodies' size
Behind two small green eyes.
The night has these—but who is this
That like a shadow glides
Across the shadows of the trees,
And his own visage hides?
He hides his face—we wonder what
That face would look like in the sun:
Perhaps an ugly bloated thing
That has more heavy chins than one;
Or is it sharp and white and thin,
With a long nose that tries to hook
Almost as sharp a chin—
And with a cold, hard, cruel look?
We cannot say, but this is sure—
If we this night saw *it*,
We'd rush to strike that monster down,
To drown him in our common spit . . .

[This man has talent . . .]

This man has talent, that man genius,
And here's the strange and cruel difference:
Talent gives pence and his reward is gold,
Genius gives gold and gets no more than pence.

A Chant

With all our mirth, I doubt if we shall be
Like Martha here, in her serenity,
When we're her age; who goes from bed to bed
To wash the faces of the newly dead;
To close their staring eyes and comb their hair,
To cross their hands and change the linen there;
Who helps the midwives[29] to give strength and breath
To babes, by almost beating them to death
With a wet towel; and half drowns them too,
Until their tender flesh is black and blue.
Not all the revels, Martha, we have been to
Can give us, when we're old, a peace like yours—
Due to the corpses you have gone and seen to.

Beggar's Song

Good people keep their holy day,
    They rest from labour on a Sunday;
But we keep holy every day,
    And rest from Monday until Monday.[30]

And yet the noblest work on earth
    Is done when beggars do their part:
They work, dear ladies, on the soft
    And tender feelings in your heart.[30]

[29] midwives [midwife 1923, 1928]
[30] [*Chorus* But we keep holy, etc. 1923]

Around that Waist[31]

Around that waist, scarce bigger than my neck,
 Where my two arms can make a double band,
That's how I'd like to hold her in a knot,
 Clasping my elbow fast with either hand.

To feel her soft round body slip and turn,
 And still to feel no bones; that clings to me,
Till she becomes at last the trembling flower
 Kissed without mercy by a powerful bee.

Her Body's a Fine House[32]

Her body's a fine house,
 Three stories I have reckoned;
Her garter marks the first,
 A belt of silk the second;
Her necklace marks the third,
 And know—before I stop—
The garden of that house
 Is planted on the top.

Oh for a Glass of Wine![33]

Oh for a glass of wine!
A glass of ruby wine, that gives the eyes
A light more wonderful than Love supplies.[34]

31 Around that Waist [Song 1923]
32 Her . . . House [Song 1923]
33 Oh . . . Wine! [no title 1923]
34 Oh . . . Love supplies. [Sung by Ralph 1923]

Oh for a glass of ale!
A glass of sparkling ale, where bubbles play
At starry heavens, and show a Milky Way.[35]

Without Contentment, what is Life?[36]

Without contentment, what is life?
  Contented minds, like bees, can suck
Sweet honey out of soot, and sleep,
  Like butterflies, on stone or rock.

Contented minds are not in towns,
  Where stars are far away and cold;
That tremble till they almost fall,
  When they draw near to Nature's world.

Such quiet nights we'll have again,
  And walk, when early morning comes,
Those dewy cemeteries, the fields—
  When they are white with mushroom tombs.

Night is the only Time I Live[37]

Night is the only time I live,
  Wherein I find delight;
For then I dream my lover's near,
  To make a day of night.

But when I wake from those sweet dreams,
  And find that he's away,
My night again begins its course,
  With every break of day.

[35] Oh . . . Milky Way. [Sung by Dick 1923]
[36] Without . . . Life? [Song 1923]
[37] Night . . . Live [Song 1923]

Who Bears in Mind[38]

Who bears in mind misfortunes gone,
    Must live in fear of more;[39]
The happy man, whose heart is light,
    Gives no such shadow power;[40]
He bears in mind no haunting past
    To start his week on Monday;[39]
No graves are written on his mind,
    To visit on a Sunday;[40]
He lives his life by days, not years,
    Each day's a life complete;[39]
Which every morning finds renewed,
    With temper calm and sweet.[41]

The Rainbow

Rainbows are lovely things:
    The bird, that shakes a cold, wet wing,
Chatters with ecstasy,
    But has no breath to sing:
No wonder, when the air
Has a double-rainbow there!

Look, there's a rainbow now!
    See how that lovely rainbow throws
Her jewelled arm around
    This world, when the rain goes!
And how I wish the rain
Would come again, and again!

[38] Who . . . Mind [Song 1923]
[39] Who . . . more;/He . . . Monday;/He . . . complete; [Sung by Dick 1923]
[40] The . . . power;/No . . . Sunday; [Sung by Dolly 1923]
[41] Which . . . sweet. [sung by Dick and Dolly 1923] Chorus: He lives his life, etc.

Love, Like a Drop of Dew

When I pass down the street and see
   The people smiling so,
It's clear enough that my true love
   Was there awhile ago.

Her lips that, following her two eyes,
   Go smiling here and there,
Seem newly kissed—but 'tis my faith
   That none but I would dare.

Love, like a drop of dew that joins
   Two blades of grass together,
Has made her mine, as I am hers,
   For ever and for ever.

Leaves

Peace to these little broken leaves,
   That strew our common ground;
That chase their tails, like silly dogs,
   As they go round and round.
For though in winter boughs are bare,
   Let us not once forget
Their summer glory, when these leaves
   Caught the great Sun in their strong net;
And made him, in the lower air,
   Tremble—no bigger than a star!

The Pond

So innocent, so quiet—yet
   That glitter in the water's eye
Has some strange meaning there, I fear;
   Did waves run wild and butt this bank
With their curled horns, when it happened here?

Beneath these heart-shaped lily-leaves,
   In water, lies a broken heart:
And one white lily in this place—
   In this deep, silent, leaf-bound pond—
Is that dead woman's upturned face.

The Meadow

Leafy with little clouds, the sky
   Is shining clear and bright.
How the grass shines—it stains the air
   Green over its own height!
And I could almost kneel for joy,
   To see this lovely meadow now:
Go on my knees for half a day,
   To kiss a handful here and there,
While babbling nonsense on the way.

Cant

What cant, oh, what hypocrisy
   Is centred in this life of man!
Self-preservation is his God,
   And has been, since his life began.

He sits to breakfast with no care
    Of others that have none;
He keeps more idle rooms than two,
    While *families* live in one;
He saves his gold, and yet he sees
    Others without a penny;
He hoards his clothes, and knows full well
    Of children without any.
He makes his own sweet life secure,
    And then—to crown all this—
Insults a God by thinking he'll
    Get everlasting bliss!

Breath

How those wet tombstones in the sun
    Are breathing silently together!
Their breath is seen, as though they lived,
    Like sheep, when out in frosty weather.
The dead beneath, that once could breathe,
    Are nothing now but breathless bones;
And is this breath the same as theirs,
    Now coming from their own tombstones?
So, when the end has come at last,
    And we're consigned to cold damp earth,
Our tombstones in the sun will show,
    By their vain breath, what ours was worth.

Down Underground

What work is going on down underground,
Without a sound—without the faintest sound!
The worms have found the place where Beauty lies,
And, entering into her two sparkling eyes,

Have dug their diamonds up; her soft breasts that
Had roses without thorns, are now laid flat;
They find a nest more comfortable there,
Than any bird could make, in her long hair;
Where they can teach their young, from thread to thread,
To leap on her white body, from her head.
This work is going on down underground,
Without a sound—without the faintest sound.

The Rabbit

Not even when the early birds
Danced on my roof with showery feet
Such music as will come from rain—
Not even then could I forget
The rabbit in his hours of pain;
Where, lying in an iron trap,
He cries all through the deafened night—
Until his smiling murderer comes,
To kill him in the morning light.

To a Lady Friend

Since you have turned unkind,
    Then let the truth be known:
We poets give our praise
    To any weed or stone,
Or sulking bird that in
    The cold, sharp wind is dumb;
To this, or that, or you—
    Whatever's first to come.

You came my way the first,
  When the life-force in my blood—
Coming from none knows where—
  Had reached its highest flood;
A time when any thing,
  No matter old or new,
Could bring my song to birth—
  Sticks, bones or rags, or you!

Note: In the 1924 printing this poem was set in italics

The Two Heavens

When, with my window opened wide at night,
To look at yonder stars with their round light,
In motion shining beautiful and clear—
As I look up, there comes this sudden fear:
That, down on earth, too dark for me to see,
Some homeless wretch looks up in misery;
And, like a man that's guilty of a sin,
I close my blinds, and draw my body in.
Still thinking of that Heaven, I dare not take
Another look, because of that man's sake;
Who in the darkness, with his mournful eyes
Has made *my* lighted home his paradise.

The Doll

Dinah is young, and I am old;
She takes two cushions to attack
Me, and her kisses close my eyes;
She combs my hair, that still is black.

Ah, my poor child, you do not know
The state of your live doll;
When you are gone out shopping, he
Sits thinking of it all.
The cushion-fights will soon be done,
He'll need a pillow for his head;
And fingers, not your kisses, love,
Must close his eyes, when he lies dead.
You'll not sit laughing on his knee
To comb his hair when white as snow,
Or when a few thin hairs remain
Of all its tangled blackness now.
Blinded by his young spirit, you
Can see no signs that he must die:
You doll, my child, will make of you
A serious woman, by and by.

Violet and Oak

Down through the trees is my green walk:
It is so narrow there and dark
That all the end, that's seen afar,
Is a dot of daylight, like a star.
When I had walked half-way or more,
I saw a pretty, small, blue flower;
And, looking closer, I espied
A small green stranger at her side.
If that flower's sweetheart lives to die
A natural death, thought I—
What will have happened by then
To a world of ever restless men?
'My little new-born oak,' I said,
'If my soul lives when I am dead,
I'll have an hour or more with you
Five hundred years from now!

When your straight back's so strong that though
Your leaves were lead on every bough,
It would not break—I'll think of you
When, weak and small, your sweetheart was
A little violet in the grass.'

Evil

How often in my dreams have I beheld
    An enemy with a grinning, loathsome face;
And then, before the dream is over, lo!
    A smiling friend has taken that enemy's place.

So, when unkindness comes my way, I think
    Of an enemy first; but in the end
It follows, two to one, the secret blow
    Is struck by one who calls himself my friend!

Call me a Nature poet, nothing more,
    Who writes of simple things, not human evil;
And hear my grief when I confess that friends
    Have tried their best to make a cunning devil!

The Poet[42]

When I went down past Charing Cross,
    A plain and simple man was I;
I might have been no more than air,
    Unseen by any mortal eye.

But, Lord in Heaven, had I the power
    To show my inward spirit there,
Then what a pack of human hounds
    Had hunted me, to strip me bare.

[42] The Poet [*no title* 1925]

A human pack, ten thousand strong,
   All in full cry to bring me down;
All greedy for my magic robe,
   All crazy for my burning crown.

A Lonely Coast[43]

A lonely coast, where sea-gulls scream for wrecks
   That never come; its desolate sides
Last visited, a hundred years ago,
   By one drowned man who wandered with the tides;
There I went mad, and with those birds I screamed,
   Till, waking, found 'twas only what I dreamed.

[Still do I claim . . .]

Still do I claim no man can reach
   His highest soul's perfection,
Until his life, from day to day,
   Deserves a dog's affection.

The Two Loves[44]

I have two loves, and one is dark,
   The other fair as may be seen;
My dark love is Old London Town,
   My fair love is the Country green.

My fair love has a sweeter breath,
   A clearer face by day; and nights
So wild with stars that dazzled I
   See multitudes of *other* lights.

[43] A Lonely Coast [*no title* 1925]
[44] The Two Loves [*no title* 1925]

My dark love has her domes, as round
   As mushrooms in my fair love's meadows;
While both my loves have houses old,
   Whose windows look cross-eyed at shadows.

No-man's Wood[45]

Shall I have jealous thoughts to nurse,
When I behold a rich man's house?
Not though his windows, thick as stars,
   Number the days in every year;
I, with one window for each month,
   Am rich in four or five to spare.

But when I count his shrubberies,
His fountains there, and clumps of trees,
Over the palings of his park
   I leap with my primeval blood;
Down wild ravines to Ocean's rocks,
   Clean through the heart of No-man's Wood.

The Life of Man[46]

All from his cradle to his grave,
Poor devil, man's a frightened fool;
His Mother talks of imps and ghosts,
His Master threatens him at school.
When half a man and half a boy,
The Law complains of his high blood;
And then the Parson threatens him
With hell, unless baptized for good.

[45] No-man's Wood [no title 1925]
[46] The Life of Man [no title 1925]

Soon after, when a married man,
He fears the humours of his Spouse;
And, when a father, fears to spend
One shilling that his Babes might lose.
Then comes Old Age, Lumbago, Gout,
Rheumatic Pains that ache and sting:
All from his cradle to his grave,
Poor devil, man's a frightened thing.

The Bust[47]

When I went wandering far from home,
I left a woman in my room
To clean my hearth and floor, and dust
My shelves and pictures, books and bust.

When I came back a welcome glow
Burned in her eyes—her voice was low;
And everything[48] was in its place,
As clean and bright as her own face.

But when I looked more closely there,
The dust was on my dark, bronze hair;
The nose and eyebrows too were white—
And yet the lips were clean and bright.

The years have gone, and so has she,
But still the truth remains with me—
How that hard mouth was once kept clean
By living lips that kissed unseen.

[47] The Bust [*no title* 1925]
[48] everything [every thing 1925]

146

[An artist draws . . .]

An artist draws his own strange mind,
    We're but his mirrors—I and you;
If he's a devil—so am I;
    If he's an angel—I'm one too.

The Treasured Three[49]

Here with my treasured Three I sit,
    Here in my little house of joy,
Sharing one fire, and on one mat:
    My wife and my dog, Beauty Boy,
And my black Venus of a cat.

But while they sleep I sit and think;
    Will Death take my black Venus first;
Shall I be first, or Beauty Boy,
    Or Dinah, whom I love the most—
To leave this little house of joy?

[This little town's a purer place]

This little town's a purer place
    Than any city, rich or poor:
Six thousand slanderous tongues, that's all—
    While London has seven millions more.

J is for Jealousy

I praised the daisies on my lawn,
And then my lady mowed them down.

[49] The Treasured Three [*no title* 1925]

My garden stones, improved by moss,
She moved—and that was Beauty's loss.
When I adored the sunlight, she
Kept a bright fire indoors for me.
She saw I loved the birds, and that
Made her one day bring home a cat.
She plucks my flowers to deck each room,
And make me follow where they bloom.
Because my friends were kind and many,
She said—'What need has Love of any?'
What is my gain, and what my loss?
Fire without sun, stones bare of moss,
Daisies beheaded, one by one;
The birds cat-hunted, friends all gone—
These are my losses: yet, I swear,
A love less jealous in its care
Would not be worth the changing skin
That she and I are living in.

Note: In the 1925 printing these poems appeared without the verb
'is' in the titles.

N is for Nature

Day after day I find some new delight:
　　It was the grass that pressed upon my cheeks,
That had a touch as soft as Death's, when he
　　Comes to a sleeping child that never wakes.

And now the wind and rain: it was the rain
　　That made the wind reveal his breath at last;
But 'twas the wind that, travelling high and far,
　　Furrowed the Heavens with clouds from East to West.

And when the night has come, perhaps the Moon,
   With her round face all shining clear and bright,
Will ride the dark, humped clouds with camels' backs—
   And end my day with that last new delight.

O is for Open

Are those small silver tumps a town,
   And are those dewdrops windows there;
Is that dark patch a hill or cloud,
   And which is Earth, and which is air?
Lord, when I see a world so vast,
   This large, bewildering stretch of land;
The far-off fields, the clumps of woods,
   The hills as thin as clouds beyond—
When I see this, I shrink in fear,
   That if I once but close my eye,
The ends will sink, and leave me dazed
   Before a monstrous, empty sky!

P is for Pool

I know a deep and lonely pool—that's where
   The great Kingfisher makes his sudden splash!
He has so many jewels in his plumes
   That all we see is one blue lightning flash.

But whether that fine bird comes there or no,
   There I'll be found before the coming night—
Beside that dark, deep pool, on whose calm breast
   Sleep a young family of pools of light.

And near my pool an ancient abbey stands,
  Where I, when lying in the longest grass,
Can see the moonlight, tender, soft and fair,
  Clasped to the rugged breast of that black nurse.

R is for Remembrance

I have no memory of his face,
  A bearded man or smooth and bare;
I never heard my mother call
  My father either dark or fair.

All I remember is a coat
  Of velvet, buttoned on his breast;
Where I, when tired of fingering it,
  Would lay my childish head and rest.

His voice was low and seldom heard,
  His body small—I've heard it said;
But his hoarse cough made children think
  Of monsters growling to be fed.

If any children took that road,
  And heard my father coughing near,
They whispered, 'Hist! Away, away—
  There's some big giant lives in there!'

S is for Swimmer

When I had crossed the hill at last,
  And reached the water's brink,
'For once, in all my life,' thought I—
  'I'll swim in water fit to drink.'

'In this calm lake, so clear and pure,
  Which has no weeds or thorns,
I'll send a thousand small blue waves
  To butt the rocks with milk-white horns.

'I'll laugh and splash till, out of breath,
  My life is almost done;
And all that's left is one wild hand
  Above me, clutching at the Sun!'

U is for Union

If Time and Nature serve us both alike,
  I shall be dead for years, when you are dying;
Remember then how much I loved the birds:
  That should you hear a gentle bird-voice crying
'Sweet! Sweet!' You'll know at once whose lover waits.
  I shall be there in all good time to show
The way that leads to a new life and home—
  Ere Death can freeze one finger-tip or toe.
But we'll have years together yet, I trust,
  In this green world: how many sparrows came
To breakfast here this morning, with the frost
  As plump as snow on window-sill and frame?

W is for Will

If I should die, this house is yours,
  A little money too:
It's but a poor reward I make,
  For all this care from you.

And though you take a second mate,
   And think that man the best,
I would not change—if dead men could—
   One word of this bequest.

Would that I could bequeath to you
   My joy in Earth and sky—
Worth more than gold or precious stones,
   To be remembered by.

X is for Expecting

Come, come, my Love, the morning waits,
What magic now shall greet our sight!
   What butterflies
   Before our eyes
Shall vanish in the open light!

Come, while the Sun has power to strike
Our household fires all dead and cold!
   How softly now
   The wind can blow—
When carrying off a field of gold!

Come, when behind some leafy hedge
We'll see a snow-white, new-born lamb
   No man has set
   His eyes on yet—
Where it lies sleeping near its dam.

Come, come, my Love, the morning waits,
The Sun is high, the dew has gone!
   The air's as bright
   As though the light
Of twelve May mornings came in one.

Z is for Zany

Why does a woman change her moods?
  That man may have no thought but hers;
When man has silent, unknown dreams,
  Oh, how it troubles her with fears:
Her words, what jealous fear they prove—
'A penny for your thoughts, my love.'

When I would think, she laughs and talks,
  That I shall know a woman's there;
She stops my hand, when it would write:
  I took her for my staff, but swear—
By every devil and every god—
This woman's love is now my rod!

from The Song of Love

LXXX

A fool without experience, poor,
  Began one day to think
How rich he'd be with scores of friends—
  And wrote that down in ink.

LXXXI

A rich man said, with scores of friends,
  Who wisely understood,
'How poor am I with these false friends!'
  And wrote that down in blood.

LXXXII

I met a lonely man who had
  No friend, no child, no wife:
O what a wretched thing, said I,
  Is this poor mortal's life!

LXXXIII

But when I met a poorer man,
  With neither friend nor foe,
This man is doubly damned, said I—
  With twice the other's woe.

LXXXIV

But Love has saved me from that state,
  I shall not live alone,
A weak, unloved, unhated thing,
  Unnoticed and unknown.

LXXXV

Though we are two are we not one?
  Aye, even as that Pair
Of scissors, which we hold in turns,
  To cut each other's hair.

LXXXVI

One—like our Pair of household tongs,
  There with his crookèd thighs,
His long thin legs, his little head
  With neither mouth nor eyes.

LXXXVII

My love is fair, but fairer still
  With eyes a little wild,
When she forgets how fair she is,
  And wonders like a child.

Let not her face be doted on
　　Too much by stranger men,
For when her back is turned their eyes
　　Dart on her ankles then. . .

Note: In the 1926 printing the numerals appeared in roman.

Hill and Vale

Day by day the man in the vale
　　Enjoyed his neighbour's hill above;
Day by day the man on the hill
　　Looked down his neighbour's vale with love.

If either one would see how fair
　　Was his own home, at any hour,
He, walking up the hill or down,
　　Enjoyed it from his neighbour's door.

So, down the vale and up the hill,
　　These neighbours travelled, to and fro;
One man to see his own green hill,
　　And one to see his vale below.

Storms

She fears not me—
　　Neither my thunder,
Nor my lightning, startles her
　　To make surrender.

But when my friend
    In Heaven makes thunder,
Her spirit breaks, and turns
    To fear and wonder.

Lightning and thunder,
    Give her no rest:
Bring her head back again,
    Back to my breast.

Old or Young[50]

I questioned Poetry, 'Say,' I said—
    'What am I, old or young?'
'Young as the heart remains,' she smiled—
    'While laughter comes, and song.'

Say, am I old or am I young?'
    I asked Philosophy.
'The way that women look at you
    Should answer that'—growled he.

So, when I claim, by my high blood,
    A life still young and jolly,
Women, with their indifferent looks
    Reprove me for my folly.

Sport

    Hunters, hunters,
    Follow the Chase.
    I saw the Fox's eyes,
    Not in his face
    But on it, big with fright—
    Haste, hunters, haste!

[50] Old or Young [Old and Young 1927]

Say, hunters, say,
Is it a noble sport?
As rats that bite
Babies in cradles, so,
Such rats and men
Take their delight.

Winter Fire

How bleak and cold the air is now—
　　The Sun has never left his bed:
He has a thick grey blanket pulled
　　All over his shoulders and head.

Big birds that only have one cry,
　　And little birds with perfect songs,
Are silent all, and work their wings
　　Much faster than they work their tongues.

I'll turn that black-faced nigger, Coal,
　　Into an Indian painted red;
And let him dance and fire wild shots
　　Into the chimney overhead.

Peace and Goodwill

On Christmas day I sit and think,
Thoughts white as snow, and black as ink.
My nearest kinsman, turned a knave,
Robbed me of all that I could save.
When he was gone, and I was poor,
His sister yelped me from her door.

The Robin sings his Christmas song,
And no bird has a sweeter tongue.
God bless them all—my wife so true,
And pretty Robin Redbreast too.
God bless my kinsman, far away,
And give his sister joy this day.

Ambition

I had Ambition, by which sin
    The angels fell;
I climbed and, step by step, O Lord,
    Ascended into Hell.

Returning now to peace and quiet,
    And made more wise,
Let my descent and fall, O Lord,
    Be into Paradise.

For Sale

Four hundred years this little house has stood
Through wind and fire, through earthquake and through
    flood;
Still its old beams, though bulged and warped, are strong,
In spite of gaping wounds both deep and long.
The doors are low and give such narrow space
We must walk humbly in this little place.
The windows here, no longer square or straight,
Are able now, from their fantastic state,
To squint down their own walls, and see the flowers
That get more drippings from the eaves than showers.
Six hundred pounds for all this precious stone!

These little, quaint old windows squinting down;
This orchard, with its apples' last appeal
To dumpling or sweet cider; this deep well,
Whose little eye has sparkled from its birth—
Four hundred years in sixty feet of earth!

Uncertainty

Shall I confess my love?
   No, no—it will not do;
Not while Uncertainty
   Can keep a woman true.
She shall not know that I,
   Being absolutely won,
Release her thousand charms
   For something new in man.
So let the game go on,
   Which Love calls 'Yes or No,'
Till Death says, 'Come with me—
   Come to a quiet show.'
Where she, or I, alone,
   Inside the cold, black vault,
Train worms to skip a hair,
   And make a somersault.

Charity

Things that are dear to me at home
   Need all my help, and more;
And many a kindly thought I kill,
   For the stranger at my door;
Yet every generous impulse slain,
   Is a ghost that haunts me still.

It's better that a woman had
   A love-child at her breast,
Than live a heartless, selfish maid;
   It's better that a man should trust
A worthless knave, than never have
   His love or innocence betrayed.

A Child's Fancy

His chin went up and down, and chewed at nothing,
His back was bent—the man was old and tired;
Toothless and frail, he hobbled on his way,
Admiring nothing, and by none admired;
Unless it was that child, with eager eyes,
Who stared amazed to see so strange a man,
And hobbled home himself, with shoulders raised
Trying to make his chin go up and down;
Unless it was that much affected child,
With rounded shoulders, like the old man seen—
Who asked his mother why he was not made
The wonderful strange sight he might have been.

A Silver Wonder

Shall I this night, amazed and full of wonder,
   Forget the Heavens and worship this new toy;
Shall I betray the stars and fall before
   A strange new Image, with a greater joy?
Caught in the searchlights' fingers, gleaming bright,
   A silver wonder, with a strange device,
Has made the stars, the great eternal stars.
   Peep out of their dark holes like timid mice!

Moss and Feather

Pools but reflect his shape and form,
  And nothing of his lovely hues;
Could he but see his jewels' light,
  Would this Kingfisher choose
To live alone with Weeping Willows,
Diving, and making toys of billows?

Her shadow shows this Stone her frame,
  But not her plumpness, round and simple;
Could she but see what moss she has,
  To jewel every dimple—
Could this rich Stone but see her face,
Would she lie idle in one place?

Were I a great Magician now,
  I'd bring this Bird and Stone together,
Lord, what a glorious pair they'd make,
  To dance, in moss and feather—
Nine times in sunshine, keeping step,
And twenty when the Moon[51] is up!

Note: This poem was printed separately as a Faber & Gwyer *Ariel* poem
  in 1928

Day or Night

Again I wake and cry for light!
  My golden day has gone,
And, looking through my window now,
  I see the stars and moon.

[51] Moon [moon 1928]

Which shall I sacrifice to sleep,
  With both beyond my praise?
So lovely are these silvery nights,
  So bright these golden days!

In Winter

The cold, ice-sucking Wind has gone,
  The air breathes quietly;
The Rain has come, as warm as spray
  That sprinkles ships at sea.

And I remember how I woke,
  Before my time to rise,
And heard a Robin and a Thrush
  Cheering the winter skies.

Now when my Summer fails to shine,
  And skies are cold and grey—
I'll let my Memory warm her hands
  At this fine winter's day.

Silver Hours

Come, lovely Morning, rich in frost
  On iron, wood and glass;
Show all your pains to silver-gild
  Each little blade of grass.

Come, rich and lovely Winter's Eve,
  That seldom handles gold;
And spread your silver sunsets out,
  In glittering fold on fold.

Come, after sunset; come, Oh come—
    You clear and frosty Night:
Dig up your fields of diamonds, till
    The heavens all dance in light!

Mangers

Who knows the name and country now,
    Of that rich man who lived of old;
Whose horses fed at silver mangers,
    And drank of wine from troughs of gold?

He who was in a manger born,
    By gold and silver undefiled—
Is known as Christ to every man,
    And Jesus to a little child.

Starlings

This time of year, when but the Robin sings,
    Shall I reproach those Starlings, chuckling near?
What Spring-like green[52] is in their feverish haste
    To pock the face of my half-ripened pear!

When I remember my own wilful blood,
    The waste, the wildness of my early years—
Shall I not chuckle with those birds, when they
    With wicked music waste my sweetest pears?

[52] green [greed 1932]

163

Wonderful Places

I am haunted by wonderful places—
And not by human faces;
My only ghosts, by day or night,
Are Nature's own, of sound or sight.
I see again the hollow, deep and round,
Filled with a murmuring sound;
Where Summer sent her flowers, with bees
And humming-birds to play with these.
Again, and still again, I dream
How Colorado's stream
Squeezed his huge body through
A narrow gorge, and never knew
That Heaven's thunder
Was but a whisper to his own down under.
Again I see the mighty leap
Made by the wild Pacific deep
At Rarotonga, off a coral bed—
With his own mist to hide his face and head.
I am haunted by wonderful places—
And not by human faces.

Trails

He leaves his silver trail behind,
    But has no silver on his way;
His path is rough, and sometimes dark,
    And troubles come by night and day:
Slowly he moves—this humble snail—
And never sees his silver trail.

So, men who give us golden lines
    Have written them in blood and sweat;
Time never turns a thought to gold,
    Unless a tear has made it wet:
They suffer—like these humble snails—
And never see their golden trails.

The Poor

Give them your silver, let the poor
    Put on a braver show;
Let not their cold and sullen looks
    Depress the world with woe.

But to the poor who laugh and sing
    Nor look depressed nor cold—
What can we give to these sweet souls,
    Worth twice their weight in gold?

A Fleeting Wonder

See where he rides, all hot and fast—
    High on his horse that kicks
Lightning and thunder out of wind,
    While fools applaud his tricks.

A year or two, and there he lies,
    A bleeding thing, and thrown;
Down in the dust he dribbles blood,
    Forgotten and unknown.

Whoa! Steady now, my little horse,
   A gentle canter past:
Though faintly cheered, there's nothing gained
   By riding wild and fast.

The Visitor

Her beauty is a wasted thing,
   She's neither sweet nor kind;
And flowers that have no other eyes
   Than raindrops soon go blind.

She is a park that has no deer
   To give it life or grace;
Until I think the wilderness
   A more enchanted place.

Her Ten Commandments are her own,
   She knows no other Creed;
The only babies in her eyes
   Are selfish thoughts and greed.

Her beauty is a wasted thing,
   Is Nature's loss and pain;
When will the little, plain, brown bird
   Come back and sing again?

Age and Youth

The music's dull—I trust my Ears;
   The day is cold—I blame no Blood;
The air is mist—I trust my Eyes;
   My breath is stale—my Teeth hold good;
My bed is hard—I blame no Bones;
   My drink is Sour—I trust my Tongue.

Ears, Blood and Eyes; Teeth, Tongue and Bones—
    Tell me what's wrong,
    And speak the truth.
'It's strange, Old man, but no complaint
    Has come from Youth.'

Jewels

Twice in one hour I've seen this lovely Night,
    Flustered at having all those jewels there—
Spilling her stars, that fall from Heaven to Earth,
    As though she carried more than she could bear.
While I, a struggling dreamer, all day long,
    That tries to polish one poor little rhyme—
Though breathed on hard, and rubbed with ecstasy,
    Still call on Night to see my wasted time.

The World Dictates[53]

The World dictates my life from day to day,
    It holds my purse, and cuts my pleasures down,
If I would ride, it tells me I must walk,
    It counts my concerts when I live in Town.
Yet when I see yon lovely hill this morning,
    All white and sepia with its trees and snow—
Who'll think I'd be a wiser, better man
    To sit in cushions at a gilded show?
So let the World dictate my daily life,
    Let beauty last till Summer brings me more—
Where lovers, paired together, laugh and play,
    As they go wobbling sideways past my door.

[53] The World Dictates [In Winter 1931]

Ourselves

We live to read each other's soul—
  We dare not read our own for shame!
But since I dare to know myself,
  Where I condemn I share the blame.

I know my very seeds of thought,
  Before they flower, or leaves are shown:
I see your fault with lazy eyes,
  To cast their lightning on my own!

Dreamers

There was a poet once who died,
His casement opened wide;
With his two hands he clasped his book,
And died with his last look
Fixed on the brightest star—
How great some poets are!
I too have my ambitious end,
With one green leaf in either hand—
And save the small breast-feather
Of a little bird for the other!

Wild Creatures

They say wild creatures hide themselves,
  And seek a quiet place to die:
Would that my end were such as theirs,
  So strange, so wild a thing am I.

Let no man sneer at me, and say—
    'We know this poet hides with care;
Inside the Abbey's sacred walls
    He hides himself—if anywhere.'

I, who have lived for Nature's love,
    Think nothing of your sculptured stones—
Who sees a dingle lined with moss,
    And one small row of clean, white bones?

Magpies

I have an orchard near my house,
    Where poppies spread and corn has grown;
It is a holy place for weeds,
    Where seeds stay on and flower, till blown.
Into this orchard, wild and quiet,
    The Magpie comes, the Owl and Rook:
To see one Magpie is not well,
    But seeing two brings all good luck.
If Magpies think the same, and say,
    'Two humans bring good luck, not one'—
How they must cheer us, Love, together,
    And tremble when I come alone!

On Finding a Dead Bird Under My Window

Here you lie, with feathers cold and wet—
To dig a grave for you will cause no sweat!
I never felt your body warm with blood,
And now I hold you longer than I should.

What does it matter, if we live or die—
You with a cherry-tempted heart, or I?
The sun in Heaven has his own heat and glow,
And, when all flesh is gone, the grass will grow.
Yet still I hope that you have left a son
Or daughter here, to do what you have done—
To tap my window sharply, without warning,
And be the first to wish a friend 'Good Morning'.

Voices of Scorn

When I had thought my end was near,
    And I must soon prepare to die—
'Be quick! Be quick!' the Mavis called,
    And 'Haw, Haw, Haw!' the Rooks did cry.

What bird, with even greater scorn,
    Has come so quickly following after?
Is this the Chaffinch—how his voice
    Reproves me with its wholesome laughter!

One Poet Visits Another

His car was worth a thousand pounds and more,
A tall and glossy black silk hat he wore;
His clothes were pressed, like pretty leaves, when they
Are found in Bibles closed for many a day;
Until the birds I love dropped something that—
    As white as milk, but thick as any cream—
Went pit, pit, pat! Right on his lovely hat!

*   *   *

Lead this unhappy poet to his car—
    Where is his longing now, where his desire?
When left alone, I'll ride him to his grave,
    On my own little horse of wind and fire.

170

My Rockery

Here in my garden I have lovely stones,
    All old and grey and some with knobs of pearl;
Stones with their silver sides, and amber backs,
    With mossy dimples and with horns that curl.

Would that this rockery were my grave indeed,
    The monument where lie my buried bones:
Though people—coming here to think of me—
    Might well forget, and stay to worship stones!

To Play Alone

A Tom Tit clinging upside down,
    Needs nothing more to raise his wonder;
A lonely Trout will play until
    His own deep whirlpool sucks him under.

So when my money all is spent,
    And all my merry friends are gone—
What little Tom Tit, Trout, or Child,
    Will teach me how to play alone?

Flying Blossoms

These Butterflies, in twos and threes,
    That flit about in wind and sun—
See how they add their flowers to flowers,
    And blossom where a plant has none!

Bring me my hat of yellow straw,
    To greet them on this summer's morn—
That they may think they see in me
    Another crop of golden corn!

A Bright Day

My windows now are giant drops of dew,
    The common stones are dancing in my eyes;
The light is winged, and panting, and the world
    Is fluttering with a little fall or rise.

See, while they shoot the sun with singing Larks,
    How those broad meadows sparkle and rejoice!
Where can the Cuckoo hide in all this light,
    And still remain unseen, and but a voice?

Shall I be mean, when all this light is mine?
    Is anything unworthy of its place?
Call for the rat, and let him share my joy,
    And sit beside me here, to wash his face.

Breast to Breast

What strange commotion, Love,
    Is seen on yonder bough?
'It's only a bird,' said she—
    'Or little winds that blow.'
Only a bird, my Love?
    Who sees the best—
When bird and leaf together
    Are fluttering breast to breast!

Eyes

The owl has come
    Right into my house;
He comes down the chimney,
    To look for a mouse—
And he sits on the rim of my old black table.

Lord, since I see
    Those wonderful eyes,
As big as a man's
    Or a maiden's in size—
Have I not proved his wisdom is no fable?

The River Severn

This is the morning bright and clear,
    To stand on top of Christchurch Hill;
We'll see the Severn, looking down,
    In all his silver beauty, Love—
Where he lies basking in the sun.

My lovely Severn shines as bright
    As any moon on trucks of coal,
Or sun above our greenest meadow;
    Till I again defy the world
To search his face and find a shadow.

Bells

The Worlds march on and circle in their place,
Thousands of Worlds march on through Time and Space;
Each World a bell that, with its different toll,
The Master strikes to One Harmonious Whole.
His ears are keen, and He can always tell
If any World rings false, and name the bell.
And even I, with all these birds in song,
And grass all round me growing green and long;
Yes, even I—though shadows mark the Moon—
Could name the guilty World that's out of tune.

The Man of Moods

Sometimes I blow and praise a bubble,
  And then I stab, to break its light;
This morning I despised a lamb,
  And now a rat would please my sight.
Lately I called my birth divine,
  And kings came second; now, my Soul
Takes penance in the cold, dark earth,
  In a cell with the snail and a mole.
To-day I love; to-morrow rue't:
Your prophet, sage and friend—the Poet.

Love and Money

I count my pounds as three times two,
  And five times one, my shillings;
Six pounds, five shillings for my Love,
  To buy a coat with frillings.

But as she takes the light and air,
  So will she take my money;
And all the thanks I'll get will be
  A quiet—'Kiss me, Honey'.

And so I will, at such a rate
  That, long before it's over—
A deer pursued by fire and wind
  Shall fly to safer cover!

To-night

What can I find in the city shops,
  To please your pretty eyes to-night;

A lovely gown that's made of silk,
   Soft to the hand, and gossamer-light?
A little book with silver clasps,
   With golden words on all its pages?
Two bowls of glass, wherein the lights
   Flit here and there, like birds in cages?
A dog to wind up like a clock,
   That's made to growl, and then to yap?
Or Cupid as a fountain, made
   To piddle in his mother's lap?

Married Couples

When Love is strong in married couples,
   They grow in looks like one another;
Till strangers think they see a son,
   And then a daughter, of one mother.

Come, Time, and make us look like twins,
   My wife, my sister, I her brother;
That this amazing proof may show
   How she and I have loved each other!

Love Lights His Fire

Love lights his fire to burn my Past—
   There goes the house where I was born!
And even Friendship—Love declares—
   Must feed his precious flames and burn.

I stuffed my life with odds and ends,
   But how much joy can Knowledge give?
The World my guide, I lived to learn—
   From Love, alone, I learn to live.

Past and Present

I who have seen a tiny cloud,
   No bigger than my Lady's puff,
Powder the Heavens with miles of soot,
   And make the seas all wild and rough;

I who have seen that speck at last
   Sink half a fleet and drown its men,
With waves, like eagles, swooping down
   To carry off both sheep and pen;

I who have felt and seen all this,
   And trained my thoughts to quiet scorn—
Am still the man to dress Love's finger,
   Scratched by a little pin or thorn.

Note: In the 1933 printing this poem had no stanza breaks.

Competitors

I had a friend to smoke and drink,
   We dined at clubs and saw the Play;
Till Love came, like the smallest wind,
   And looked him quietly away.

So Friendship goes, and Love remains,
   And who can question which is best—
A Friendship reared on the bottle, or
   A Love that's reared at the breast?

The Ghost

Seek not to know Love's full extent,
    For Death, not Life, must measure Love;
Not till one lover's dead and gone,
    Is Love made strong enough to prove.
What woman, with a ghostly lover,
    Can hold a mirror to her hair?
A man can tell his love with tears,
    When but a woman's ghost is there.
Our greatest meeting is to come,
    When either you or I are lost:
When one, being left alone in tears,
    Confesses to the other's ghost.

Pecking

One kiss to open up the day,
    One kiss at night to close it fast;
Sometimes a kiss or two between,
    To help the first and last.
But when I woke this morning early,
    I caught her pecking at my face;
Greedy for grain, she pecked and pecked
    All over the golden place.
And artful I, still feigning sleep,
    Lay quiet, while that little chick
Enjoyed the grain Love scattered there—
    And still went on to peck.

Good and Evil

A wealth of stars in Winter time
  Brings frost severe and cold;
And Winter's coppers are no more
  Than Autumn's wasted gold:
While Love herself, this very morning,
Scorned me without one word of warning.

Had I not seen a Bumble-bee
  Stand on his head in clover;
Parting the folds with hairy legs,
  For comfort under cover;
Had I not seen this Bee and wondered—
Could I have left Love's scorn unpondered?

Let Us Lie Close

Let us lie close, as lovers should,
  That, if I wake when barn-cocks crow—
I'll feel your body at my side,
  And hear your breathing come and go.

When dreams, one night, had moved our bodies,
  I, waking, listened for your breath;
I feared to reach and touch your face,
  That it was icy-cold in death.

Let us lie close, as lovers should,
  And count our breaths, as some count sheep;
Until we say 'Good night', at last,
  And with one kiss prepare for sleep.

Stings

Though bees have stings, I doubt if any bee
   Has ever stung a flower in all his life:
Neither, my love, can I think ill of you,
   Though half the world and I may be at strife.

Can I forget your coming, like the Moon
   When, robed in light, alone, without a star,
She visits ruins; and the peace you brought,
   When I with all the world was still at war.

A Lullaby of Rest

Workhouse and Bedlam, Refuge, Den,
   For Passions deaf and blind—
How many strange and peevish things
   Have harboured in my mind!

Ambition, Pride and Greed, with all
   The Body's Appetites,
Knocked at my door for lodgings, and
   Disturbed my days and nights.

Till, treading softly, like a bird,
   When young ones fill her nest—
Love sits beside me here, and sings
   A lullaby of rest.

Beauty and Brain

When I was old, and she was young,
   With all the beauty hers—
I wooed her with a silver tongue,
   With music for her ears;

And shall I now complain to find
That Beauty has so small a mind?

If this young Chit had had more sense
  Would she have married me?
That she gave me the preference,
  Proved what a fool was she:
Then let me die if I complain
That Beauty has too small a brain.

The Tyrants

Love came about the Cuckoo's time,
  Two months ago, or more;
In April I was rich in joy,
  But June has left me poor.

Love cried for money all day long,
  For more than I possessed;
The Cuckoo, making echoes fast,
  Destroyed my quiet rest.

Now, in July, in this dead calm,
  When both are gone away—
I sit alone, a peevish man,
  And miss them every day.

His Throne

When Love has lost his bite and sting,
  And all his fire has gone—
What other god shall take his place,
  And fill his golden throne?

Where Love has sat, there let him lie,
    Whether he lives or dies;
Still on that throne, where none succeeds,
    Embalmed in memories.

The Faithful One

The bird that fills my ears with song,
    The Sun that warms me with his fire;
The dog that licks my face and hands,
    And She whose beauty I desire—
Each of these think that he or she
Creates in me the joy they see.

But when my dog's gone off with a bitch,
    And there's no Sun, nor bird in song;
When Love's false eyes seek other men,
    And leave me but her lying tongue;
Still will my Joy—though forced to roam—
Remember me and come back home.

The Birth of Song

I am as certain of my song,
    When first it warms my brain,
As woman of her unborn child,
    Or wind that carries rain.
The child and rain are born at last,
    Though now concealed from sight—
So let my song, unshaped and crude,
    Come perfect to the light.

Man

Come, let us measure
   The greatness of Man;
The marvellous things on earth
   Conceived and done.

He who would measure
   How little is Man,
Must cry himself to sleep,
   Like some lost Little One.

All's Well

The cat has her milk,
   The dog has his bone;
The man has his ale,
   And his week's work is done,
He sits at a fire,
   And he sees his young wife
Give suck to her babe—
   All's well with his life.

Street Criers
(Written for Music)

When Poll stays here, her Jack goes there,
   To earn their provender;
Her cries are all in Bethnal Green—
   'Sweet Lavender! Sweet Lavender!
Who'll buy Sweet Lavender?'

And oft she wonders if her Jack
    Enjoys a man's success;
Who cries on top of Stamford Hill—
    'Young Watercress! Young Watercress!
Who'll buy Young Watercress?'

The Conquerors

Who are these men with quiet smiles—
    How came these two together?
I'd walk ten miles to meet with one
    Or ten to miss the other.

The one man smiles because the World
    Is conquered by his love;
The other smiles because the World
    Must fear his every move.

Named

As I marched out one day in Spring,
    Proud of my life and power—
I saw an infant, all alone,
    Kissing a small, red flower.
He looked at me with solemn eyes,
    As only children can,
And—in a voice that might be God's—
    He called distinctly—'Man!'
Though I had been the Pope of Rome,
    Our English King or Heir,
A child has called in God's own way,
    And I have answered—'Here!'

Song of the Miners

When starving cattle see
Their blades of grass
Locked up in ice that cuts
Their mouths, like glass—
What can they do but lie in heaps and die?

And shall our people starve,
Like these wild herds?
We, with our power to think,
Our gift of words—
Shall we lie down like these dumb brutes and die?

Good Friends

I brought two friends to share my fire,
To crack a joke or two;
I kissed one friend, and smacked my lips,
And sighed, as lovers do.
And never think, when I had slept
And, waking, found them gone—
That I abused my absent friends,
To find myself alone.
Now, shall I call my friends by name,
That shared this fire of mine?
Well, one was called 'Young Walnuts', and
The other was 'Old Wine'.

The Loneliest Mountain

The loneliest mountain, with no house or tree,
Still has its little flower so sweet and wild;
While I, a dreamer, strange and but half known,
Can find no equal till I meet a child.

The Load of Pearls

Will no one stop that Blackbird now,
    Before he sings himself to death?
Tell him there is no life on earth
    Enjoys an everlasting breath.

He sings because a tree in May
    Is flower all over, low and high:
A cherry tree, whose load of pearls
    Brings diamonds into every eye!

Taking Stock

A pipe to smoke, and ale that's mulled,
    With walnuts fresh enough to peel;
The voice of Love, that comes and goes,
    And brings a kiss between each meal;
A day that's hot, for a shady tree,
    A night that's cold, for a cosy bed;
A brain that starved for lovelier dreams,
    A body light, and daintily fed;
A search for keys no man can find,
    To turn the lock of Life and Death:
With these my stock, my song is done—
    And, tell me, do I waste my breath?

Worms

Silkworms have dressed the fairest women,
    Glowworms have their own starry climes;
Straight from his breakfast on a worm,
    The bird begins his morning chimes.

Maggots, so fat and short,
Tapeworms, so thin and long:
   'All these are able'—
Say Anglers, when they speak the truth—
   'To fill a bowl with fish for some man's table.'

A Cat's Example

For three whole days I and my cat
Have come up here, and patiently sat—
   We sit and wait on silent Time;
He for a mouse that scratched close by,
At a hole where he sets his eye—
   And I for some music and rhyme.

Is this the Poet's secret, that
He waits in patience, like this cat,
   To start a dream from under cover?
A cat's example, too, in love,
With Passion's every trick and move,
   Would burn up any human lover.

Trust

Once I was wise when, in my Youth,
   I went my way alone;
Before this world betrayed my trust,
   And turned my heart to stone.

Or is it all in God's good time,
   In keeping with His plan—
That I may put more trust in Him,
   The more I lose in Man?

Common Joys

See how those diamonds splutter and choke—
    What greedy things they are for light!
That pearl, whose pulse less wildly beats,
    Is far more restful to my sight.
Soon tired of all these glittering toys,
    With my delight and wonder gone—
I send my thoughts, like butterflies,
    To dream on some old spotted stone.

So, when the Skylark sings no more,
    And I have seen the graceful Swallow;
When I have heard the Blackbird too,
    And many a bird in field or furrow:
Then to my Sparrow I return,
    Who scolds me well for what he misses—
And thinks a common chirp at times
    Pays all his debts, like children's kisses.

Speed

Think, Man of Flesh, and be not proud
    That you can fly so fast:
The little Worm can creep, creep, creep,
    And catch you up at last—
Catch up with you at last.

Though you outfly the swiftest bird,
    And laugh as you go past,
Think how the Worm comes, creep, creep, creep,
    To catch you up at last—
Catch up with you at last.

Armed for War

Is life on Earth a viler thing
   Than ever was known before?
Who shall we ask—the wise old man
   Whose years have reached five score?

When we have questioned Church and State,
   Is there anyone else to ask?
Is it the Baby, three weeks old,
   That wears a gas-proof mask?

Is it the Infant armed to meet
   A poisoned earth and sky—
A thing too weak to lift its hand
   To rub a sleepy eye?

The Tugged Hand

I have no ears or eyes
   For either bird or flower;
Music and lovely blooms
   Must bide their lighter hour;
So let them wait awhile—
   For yet another day

Till I at last forget
   The woman lying dead;
And how a lonely child
   Came to his mother's bed
And tugged at her cold hand—
   And could not make it play.

All in June

A week ago I had a fire,
   To warm my feet, my hands and face;
Cold winds, that never make a friend,
   Crept in and out of every place.

To-day, the fields are rich in grass,
   And buttercups in thousands grow;
I'll show the World where I have been—
   With gold-dust seen on either shoe.

Till to my garden back I come,
   Where bumble-bees, for hours and hours,
Sit on their soft, fat, velvet bums,
   To wriggle out of hollow flowers.

The Worms' Contempt

What do we earn for all our gentle grace?
A body stiff and cold from foot to face.

If you have beauty, what is beauty worth?
A mask to hide it, made of common earth.

What do we get for all our song and prattle?
A gasp for longer breath, and then a rattle.

What do we earn for dreams, and our high teaching?
The worms' contempt, that have no time for preaching.

Nailsworth Hill

The Moon, that peeped as she came up,
 Is clear on top, with all her light;
She rests her chin on Nailsworth Hill,
 And, where she looks, the World is white.

White with her light—or is it Frost,
 Or is it Snow her eyes have seen;
Or is it Cherry blossom there,
 Where no such trees have ever been?

Looks

What knowledge do my Ears provide,
 What do I learn from books?
I trust my Eyes for what I think
 And feed on silent looks.

The things I hear with my two Ears
 Still cry aloud for proof;
But what I see with my two Eyes
 Must be the very truth.

The woman that's behind my back,
 To hide her looks from me—
Knows not the face of him I watch
 Stirs to her treachery.

That Golden Time

When will it come, that golden time,
  When every man is free?
Men who have power to choose their tasks
  Have all their liberty.

They'll sweat and toil who love to feel
  Their muscles swell and move;
While men whose minds are more to them,
  Create the dreams we love.

When will it come, that golden time,
  When every heart must sing?
The power to choose the work we love
  Makes every man a king.

INDEX OF TITLES AND FIRST LINES

Titles are given in italics

199